The Perennial Philosophy
Series

World Wisdom
The Library of Perennial Philosophy

The Library of Perennial Philosophy is dedicated to the exposition of the timeless Truth underlying the diverse religions. This Truth, often referred to as the *Sophia Perennis*—or Perennial Wisdom—finds its expression in the revealed Scriptures as well as in the writings of the great sages and the artistic creations of the traditional worlds.

Outline of Sufism: The Essentials of Islamic Spirituality appears as one of our selections in the Perennial Philosophy series.

The Perennial Philosophy Series

In the beginning of the twentieth century, a school of thought arose which has focused on the enunciation and explanation of the Perennial Philosophy. Deeply rooted in the sense of the sacred, the writings of its leading exponents establish an indispensable foundation for understanding the timeless Truth and spiritual practices which live in the heart of all religions. Some of these titles are companion volumes to the Treasures of the World's Religions series, which allows a comparison of the writings of the great sages of the past with the perennialist authors of our time.

OTHER WORKS BY
WILLIAM STODDART

What Does Islam Mean in Today's World?

What Do the Religions Say about Each Other?
Christian Attitudes towards Islam, Islamic Attitudes
towards Christianity

Invincible Wisdom: Quotations from the Scriptures, Saints,
and Sages of All Times and Places

Remembering in a World of Forgetting: Thoughts on
Tradition and Postmodernism

Outline of Buddhism

Outline of Hinduism

Outline of Sufism

THE ESSENTIALS OF
ISLAMIC SPIRITUALITY

William Stoddart

Foreword by
R.W. J. Austin

World Wisdom

Outline of Sufism: The Essentials of Islamic Spirituality
©2012 World Wisdom, Inc.

Cover:
Detail of "A Prince Enthroned", from a copy of the fifth book
of Rūmī's *Mathnawī*, c. 1530, Safavid period, from the court
of Shah Tahmasp (r. 1524-76); opaque watercolor, ink, and
gold on paper, Herat, Afghanistan. The image depicts a prince
witnessing a Sufi spiritual dance of the type made famous by
the Whirling Dervishes of Konya.

Library of Congress Cataloging-in-Publication Data

Stoddart, William.
    Outline of Sufism : the essentials of Islamic spirituality / Wil-
liam Stoddart ; foreword by R. W. J. Austin.
        p. cm. -- (The perennial philosophy series)
    Includes bibliographical references and index.
    ISBN 978-1-936597-02-4 (pbk. : alk. paper) 1. Sufism. I.
Austin, R. W. J. II. Title.
    BP189.S74 2012
    297.4--dc23
                                                2011050000

Printed on acid-free paper in the United States of America

For information address World Wisdom, Inc.
P.O. Box 2682, Bloomington, Indiana 47402-2682
www.worldwisdom.com

Verily We (God) have raised in every nation a Messenger, proclaiming: Serve God and shun false gods.

Koran, *Sūra* "The Bee", 16:36

We (God) make no distinction between any of them [the prophets].

Koran, *Sūra* "The Cow", 2:136

We (God) caused Jesus, son of Mary, to follow them [the Hebrew prophets], and gave him the Gospel, and placed compassion and mercy in the hearts of those who follow him.

Koran, *Sūra* "Iron", 57:27

Verily, those who believe [i.e. Muslims], those who are Jews, Sabeans, and Christians, and whosoever believeth in the Last Day and doeth good: no fear shall come upon them, nor shall they grieve.

Koran, *Sūra* "The Table", 5:69

You will find that the best friends of believers [i.e. Muslims] are those who say: "We are Christians." This is because there are priests and monks amongst them, and because they are not proud.

Koran, *Sūra* "The Table", 5:82

*
* *

My heart has become capable of every form: it is a pasture for gazelles, a cloister for Christian monks, a temple for idols, the Kaaba of the pilgrim, the tablets of the Torah, and the Book of the Koran. I practice the religion of Love. In whatsoever directions its caravans advance, the religion of Love shall be my religion and my faith.

Muhyi 'd-Dīn ibn 'Arabī (1165-1240)

I am neither Christian nor Jew nor Parsi nor Muslim. I am neither of the East nor of the West, neither of the land nor of the sea. . . . I have put aside duality and have seen that the two worlds are one. I seek the One, I know the One, I see the One, I invoke the One. He is the First, He is the Last, He is the Outward, He is the Inward.

Jalāl ad-Dīn Rūmī (1207-1273)

CONTENTS

LIST OF ILLUSTRATIONS

Color Illustrations of Islamic Art and Architecture

Black-and-White Illustrations in the Text

Tables and Diagrams

NOTE ON TRANSLITERATION

In the transliteration of Arabic words the most generally accepted method has been used throughout. Following the custom of the earlier Arabists, the *tā marbūta* has been transliterated as *a*, except where a vowel follows, thus: *sūra*, but *Sūrat aḍ-Ḍuḥā* (or *Sūratu' ḍ-Ḍuḥā*); likewise the terminal *hamza* has not been transliterated except where a vowel follows, thus: *fanā*, but *fanā'al-fanā* (or *fanā'u 'l-fanā'i*).

In Arabic, certain consonants exist in two forms. In transliteration, one of the two forms in each of these cases, is customarily indicated by a dot underneath the letter. This custom has not been observed throughout this book, except on this page and in the section in the Introduction headed "Exoterism and Esoterism", where this distinction is necessary in order to make a linguistic point.

FOREWORD

Few would today dispute that we live in an age marked, as
few others have been, by a prevailing spiritual confusion
and ambiguity. One of the principal effects of this state
of affairs has been an unprecedented outpouring of the
printed word on the subject of religion in general and
mysticism in particular, which is a manifestation at once
of a deep spiritual hunger and of the rampant mental
curiosity so characteristic of secularized man.

However, since the outward forms and doctrines
of established religion have become "outmoded and
discredited" in this post-liberal age, the concern of many
of the more recent exponents of religious wisdom has
been to isolate the mystical, and therefore the apparently
less formal, aspects of the major religious traditions
and present them, out of context, as newly discovered
"philosophies for our times". This practice of attempting
to cream off from the major religions material considered
acceptable and palatable to a secularized reading public
is ill-conceived, deceptive, and dangerous, since it
leads people to imagine that they are able, without the
necessary doctrinal and psychological training, to acquire
the spiritual blessing and benefit intended only for those
whose commitment is to the particular tradition as a
whole.

This phenomenon is manifest in the many pseudo-oriental cults which now abound in the main urban centers of the Western world. Although, until recently, interest of this kind has been largely restricted to various aspects of Hindu and Buddhist spirituality, Sufism, the mystical tradition of Islam, has now also become an object of curiosity and re-adaptation, and this book on Sufism is to be welcomed as a corrective to much muddled thinking on the subject.

There are various ways in which one may approach the study of Islamic mysticism. Firstly, there is the approach of the Sufi himself, who regards his Way or Method as the true expression of Islamic spirituality which, as such, began with the Prophet Mohammed and has been part and parcel of the spiritual tradition of Islam as a whole ever since. To study Sufism from purely Sufi sources, however, assumes a thorough acquaintance with Islamic religion in general and also preferably a grasp of one of its native languages.

Secondly, one may study the many works of scholarship produced over the last seventy-five years or so by Western orientalists, much of it painstaking and highly informative, but often lacking in an appreciation of the experiential flavor of Sufism so essential for any proper understanding. Also, this approach is usually committed to the notion, variously expressed, that Sufism is something essentially alien to Islam which has been grafted onto it by borrowing from other religions.

Lastly, there is what may be termed the universalist approach, which regards Islam and Sufism as a particular manifestation of universal human aspirations towards the supernatural and spiritual. This approach can be extremely useful and illuminating, especially in these times, when an exposition of fundamental principles and symbols can guide the seeker through the profusion of religions and cults which are now offered to him. This is particularly true of the valuable work of René Guénon, Frithjof

Schuon, and Titus Burckhardt who, while perceiving the spiritual essentials common to all the great religious traditions, do not make the mistake, so often made by others, of belittling the significance and importance of a definite and unequivocal commitment to one particular tradition, nor do they forget the truth that the individual is molded by a religious tradition and not vice versa.

For, just as the universalist approach can be of great help to present-day seekers, it can, in the wrong hands, be extremely misleading, since there are two ways in which this approach can be misused. It is an approach often adopted by secular scholars, particularly anthropologists and sociologists, who tend to study all religions as universally primitive and outmoded attempts on the part of pre-scientific man to comprehend the universe and his place in it. In other words, they reject the validity and truth of all religions, except as interesting specimens for "objective" scrutiny. A universalist approach is also adopted by the host of mystic cult peddlers who take refuge in a vague, blurring universalism in order to conceal their unwillingness to submit or commit themselves to the spiritual, mental, and psychological obligations incumbent upon any genuine seeker after truth.

Dr. Stoddart has produced a work on Sufism which provides the serious reader with a true universalist approach, in that he has kept firmly and distinctly in view the Islamic nature and context of Sufism, while employing comparisons with other religious traditions where such comparison illuminates common fundamental principles and does not obscure real and providential differences of spiritual perspective, a consideration of crucial importance in any legitimate study of the religions of the world.

R.W.J. Austin
Senior Lecturer in Arabic (Retired)
School of Oriental Studies,
University of Durham, England

The Divine Name (*Allāh*)
surrounded by verses from the Koran
(from a Moroccan woodcut)

INTRODUCTION

No Sufism without Islam

For many years, there has been a growing tendency for people to say "I do not believe in religion, I believe in spirituality". One may wonder what "spirituality" can mean for these people, for this assertion indicates an unawareness of the meaning of the two terms, and of the mutual relationship between the two realities which the terms signify. This lack of awareness, in the case of a matter of such importance, cannot but have negative results for both the individual and the community.

It seems that people prefer "spirituality" because what they regard as such puts few demands on their minds, and little restraint on their egos. On the contrary, it allows their minds to wander at will, and it opens the way for the indulgence of any wayward desires. What may be called the "objective element" in religion goes by default. It has been forgotten that the great revealed religions, with their time-honored teachings of wisdom and salvation, with their intellectual requirements, and their moral restraints, cannot be cast aside without the dire consequences for society that we already see all around us.

By "religion", these people appear to mean what they call "dogmatic" and "formalistic" religion. Unfortunately, it has to be immediately conceded that almost all traditional

1

and formal religion has now been thoroughly denatured and emptied of content.[1] Whatever remains is subjective, fluctuating, arbitrary, and lacking in the dignity, authority, and permanence which are the hallmark of true religion. But, alas, it is precisely these venerable attributes (in fact now lacking in the organized religion of today) which the people referred to specifically reject. Let it be said at this point that this contemporary denaturing of religion has also, in a variety of ways, affected and grievously wounded all of the great world religions. Nevertheless, it is true to say that in each one of them there are stalwart pockets of resistance, however small, where the age-old beliefs and spiritual practices are still honored. Religion may well be "outward" and formal, but its co-relative, spirituality, is "inward" and supra-formal. Each element plays an indispensable role, and the relationship between the two needs to be clearly understood and preserved.

There is however another cause for the "spirituality" of today, and it is as follows: Given that formal religion is now largely devoid of truly spiritual content, and also that there is no longer any teaching of traditional Protestantism or Catholicism in the schools, a spiritual vacuum is automatically created. Given further that there are many

[1]   In Catholicism, this was brought about by the Vatican II Council (1962-65), the desacralizing and relativizing effects of which gradually spread to the other mainline denominations; in Islam, it was brought about by the "Islamic revolution" of Khomeini in Iran and the "Islamic republic" of Gadhafi in Libya.

The term "fundamentalism", attributed to these two revolutions, is somewhat misleading; at best, one would have to say *false* fundamentalism, because they have strayed far from the true "fundaments", or principles, of Islam. For a review of the different categories of Muslims in today's world, see my book *What Does Islam Mean in Today's World?*, chap. 4.

good people who feel a need to fill this vacuum with something real, it results that there are now many people, young and old, who are "looking for something". (Those who are not, are already dead!) Since the arguments offered by the small and still authentic Christian groups are now, for most people, no longer sufficient to pierce through the multiple layers of illusion of the scientific age, it is understandable that many people turn, in good faith and with sincere hopes, to what can only be called an ill-defined "spirituality". One can give much sympathy to those who are facing this predicament, for what on earth is available for them today?

All that this book on Sufism (and, indirectly and implicitly, on other traditional systems of spirituality) can offer is the ancient counsel: "Seek and ye shall find; knock, and it shall be opened unto you" (Matt. 7:7). This must obviously be done with perseverance and humility. Contemporary seekers have a lot to learn and a lot to gain. This counsel is one of hope, not of despair.

The inward dimension of formal religion is "mysticism",[2] and the mysticism of Islam is Sufism. Mysticism makes its appearance within every religion, and to attempt to separate the mystical element from the religion which is its outward support is an act of violence which cannot but be fatal to the mysticism, or spiritual path, concerned. Mysticism relies on the respective outward form for its objective expression, its stability, its guarantee of orthodoxy ("right thinking"), and its traditional symbolism. Many have wanted to be a Yogi without being a Hindu, and many have wanted to be a Sufi without being a Muslim. It is a vain endeavor. One

[2] From the Greek *mystēs*, which means one who has been initiated into (and sworn to secrecy regarding) one of the ancient Greek mystery cults.

might as well seek to have a human life without a human body. To be sure, the body (though made in the image of God) is corruptible and mortal, whereas life is invisible and immortal. Nevertheless, as far as we in this world are concerned, it is only in the body that life finds its support and expression. It is analogous in the case of mysticism, and the lives of all the great mystics bear witness to this— quite irrespective of the fact that it can be said of them that they are inwardly free and "above outward forms".[3] One cannot be a Benedictine monk without being a Christian, or a Sufi without being a Muslim. There can be no Sufism without the corresponding religion of Islam.

Exoterism and Esoterism[4]

In Islam these two domains—outward and inward—are more or less distinct, though they bear a clear relationship to one another. This relationship is traditionally described as follows: the outward religion, or "exoterism" (known in Islam as the *sharī'a*), may be likened to the circumference of a circle. The inner Truth, or "esoterism" (known as the *haqīqa*) that lies at the heart of the religion, may

---

[3] "Above", not "below". It is precisely those who "do not believe in formal religion", who are "below" outward forms, and who, in fact, need them most.

[4] As regards the pronunciation of the words "exoterism" and "esoterism" (used throughout the book), let it be said that the emphasis falls on the second syllable. These forms have been preferred to the alternatives "exotéricism" and "esotéricism" in which the emphasis falls on the third syllable. In the case of the adjectives "exotéric" and "esotéric", the emphasis falls on the third syllable. The pattern for the correct placing of the emphasis in "exóterism" and "esóterism" and the corresponding adjectives is provided by the terms "metábolism" and "metabólic".

4

be likened to the circle's center. The radius proceeding from circumference to center represents the mystical or "initiatic" path (called the *tarīqa*) that leads from outward observance to inward conviction, from belief to vision, and, in scholastic terms, from potency to act. The complete religion thus comprises *sharī'a*, *haqīqa*, and *tarīqa*. The *sharī'a* and the *tarīqa* will each have its own particular character, with aspects either contingent and relative or essential and absolute. Only the *haqīqa* is pure Essence and pure Absoluity.

In Arabic, Sufism is called *taṣawwuf*. This word comes from *ṣūf* ("wool"), a reference to the woolen robe worn by the earliest Sufis. Since early times some have also linked the word *ṣūfī* with *ṣūfīya* ("purified" or "chosen" [by God]"). The connection with the Greek *sophia* ("wisdom"), however, is generally regarded as no more than a pious pun, since the Greek letter *sigma* is regularly transliterated by the Arabic letter *sīn*, and not by *ṣād* as in *ṣūfī*. It is interesting to note, however, that in much later times, the Turks transliterated Hagia Sophia (the Church of the Holy Wisdom in Istanbul) as *Aya Ṣūfīya*, replacing here the Greek *sigma* with the letter *ṣād*.[5]

Strictly speaking, the Arabic word *ṣūfī*, like the Sanskrit word *yogi*, refers only to one who has attained the goal; nevertheless, it is often applied by extension to initiates who are still merely traveling towards it. The word "initiate" serves to indicate that, in order to embark on the spiritual path, a special rite of initiation is an indispensable prerequisite. More will be said about this later.

From the foregoing it will be seen that Sufism (*tasawwuf*) comprises two elements: *haqīqa* and *tarīqa*,

---

[5] For a full discussion of this question, see "The Necessity for the Rise of the Term Sufi" by Victor Danner in *Studies in Comparative Religion*, London, Spring 1972.

esoterism and initiation, intellectuality and spirituality, doctrine and method.

The *sharī'a*, for its part, supplies the necessary traditional framework; it is the "outward religion" which is accessible to, and indispensable for, all; *Tasawwuf*, on the other hand, is only for those possessed of the necessary vocation. In practice, therefore, it cannot but be the affair of a minority, though it may sometimes have popular manifestations.

Classification of the Religions

For certain historical and other reasons, Hinduism and Buddhism have always been more familiar to Westerners than is Islam. It can fairly be said that Islam is "the unknown religion". It is not only that there is a widespread ignorance of the true nature of Islam, there is also, as a result of the "Islamic" terrorists, a widespread hostility. In view of this, it may be useful to digress for a moment, and consider the classification of the religions, so that, before we go any further, Islam's place amongst them may be better understood.

Firstly, one may look at the religions from a simple geographical point of view. The religion of the Far East is, predominantly, Buddhism—Mahāyāna (or "Greater Vehicle") in Tibet, China, and Japan, and Hīnayāna[6] (or "Lesser Vehicle") in Sri Lanka, Burma, Thailand, and Cambodia. In the Indian sub-continent, the predominant religion, covering three-quarters of the total population, is Hinduism. In the Middle East, Near East, and North Africa, as well as in the northern parts of the Indian sub-continent, the religion of the overwhelming majority is

---

[6] The only school of Hīnayāna which is still extant is Theravāda ("The Primitive Way").

Islam. (In this connection, however, one must never forget the "Far Eastern" Islam of Malaysia and Indonesia, and the "African" Islam of Africa south of the Sahara.) In Europe, of course, the religion is Christianity: Orthodoxy, largely, in the East, Catholicism, largely, in the South West, and Protestantism, largely in the North West.

From a somewhat deeper point of view, one may look at the religions according to their type. Thus we have the diverse branches of Hyperborean shamanism: Taoism, Confucianism, Shinto, Bön (the pre-Buddhist religion of Tibet), Siberian shamanism, and the religion of the Sun Dance and the Sacred Pipe (the religion of the North American Indians); then we have the Aryan mythologies: Hinduism, Buddhism, Jainism, Zoroastrianism or Parsiism, and the now extinct Greco-Roman, Nordic, and Celtic religions; and finally we have the Semitic monotheisms (ultimately stemming from Abraham): Judaism, Christianity, and Islam.

The latter is probably the most useful of the classifications; but there are certain relationships which cross the frontiers of the three categories mentioned. Thus Buddhism, Christianity, and Islam are "universal" religions, each one seeking converts, claiming the allegiance of peoples everywhere, while Hinduism and Judaism are both the religions of a single people (or a group of peoples). Then again, Hinduism, Buddhism, and Christianity have a similarity in that they are all "incarnationist", and thus modify, in this respect, the "strict" monotheism, of Judaism and Islam. Buddhism, for its part, enjoys the distinction of being the only "non-theistic" religion— not atheistic, of course, since like the other religions it is based on the idea of a transcendent Absolute (the "Buddha" or "Buddhahood"); the key to the latter is *Nirvāna* ("extinction"—in Western terms, "self-naughting" or *vacare Deo*).

Mankind may be looked at either from the point of view of its differentiation or from that of its equality. The hierarchical differentiation of mankind finds expression in Hinduism (with its four castes: *brahmins, kshatriyas, vaishyas, shūdras*) and, analogously, in Christendom, with its four estates: Lords Spiritual (the spiritual hierarchy), Lords Temporal (kings, nobles), the "middle class" (craftsmen, farmers, and merchants), and serfs. From this point of view, men are manifestly unequal, and hierarchy goes hand in hand with heredity. The role of heredity is precisely the preservation and perpetuation of quality. Not only the color of one's eyes, but also intelligence and character are passed on from one generation to another. It should not be forgotten that with the privileges of birth go obligations. *Noblesse oblige.*

Islam, on the other hand, emphasizes human equality. This shows itself both positively and negatively: firstly, man's "theomorphic" nature is common to all, and secondly, the wretchedness of man's terrestrial exile is shared by prince and commoner alike: all human beings are inescapably faced with suffering, and all human beings must die. Buddhism also takes this point of view. Equality is thus as inherent to mankind as is hierarchy; and one, just as much as the other, may be the basis of a religious perspective.

Whether it be hierarchy or equality that predominates in a given religion, the other point of view is also implicitly and actually present. Thus, in Christianity, in spite of its four estates, it is fundamental that all men are "created in the image of God" (Gen. 1:27);[7] and, in Hinduism, no one asks the *sannyāsin* what was his caste before he became a pilgrim or a monk. On the other hand, in Islam, the religion

---

[7] Not "equal", which is ridiculously untrue.

of equality, the phenomenon of heredity finds expression in the existence of the *shurafā* (singular *sharīf*) who are the descendants of the Prophet. These people possess no specific "caste" function, but enjoy certain innate spiritual privileges.

Finally we may note that, whereas Hinduism is the oldest of the religions, Islam is the youngest.

CHAPTER 1

ISLAMIC EXOTERISM (*Sharī'a*)

As already noted, Islam is the third of the three Semitic monotheisms. It has its origin in the revelation which Mohammed, a scion of a noble Arab tribe (the Quraish) settled in seventh century Mecca, received from God through the intermediary of the Archangel Gabriel. This revelation came upon Mohammed when he was in middle life, and he made it known progressively to his companions over a number of years. These intermittent utterances of the revelation were subsequently committed to writing, and constitute the Koran,[1] the sacred book of Islam. For Islam, the Koran is the direct and immediate Word of God.

The language of the Koran is Arabic, which is the sacred language of Islam. As such, it occupies an even more fundamental position in Islam than do the various liturgical languages (Latin, Greek, Slavonic, etc.) in Christianity. Its role is more comparable to that of Sanskrit in Hinduism or Hebrew in Judaism. It is significant that Arabic is

---

[1] From the Arabic *Qur'ān*, "recitation".

the most archaic of all the living Semitic languages: its morphology is to be found in Hammurabi's code,[2] which is more or less contemporary with Abraham. The words of the Koran have been faithfully preserved in the form in which they were originally received, even down to the minutest points of detail, and their recitation constitutes a "liturgical" act. For this purpose only the original Arabic may be used, as translations have no liturgical validity.

Being the "uncreated Word of God", it is the Koran, and not Mohammed, which is at the center of the Islamic religion. This contrasts outwardly with Christianity, where it is Christ, and not the New Testament, who is at the center. This contrast is purely outward, however, as in Christianity Christ is, precisely, the "uncreated Word of God", and thus, in this respect, there is a far-reaching inward analogy. Herein lies the reason why an adherent of Christianity (which is centered on Christ) is called a "Christian", whereas an adherent of Islam (which is not, in the first instance, centered on Mohammed) is not properly designated by the term "Mohammedan"[3] but by the term "Muslim", which means "one who submits"; "Islam" means "submission" (i.e. to God).

In Christianity, Christ is "true Man and true God". Using the same terminology, one could say that in Islam Mohammed is "true Man" only. As we have seen, it is the Koran and not Mohammed, that is divine. As Frithjof

---

[2] See Édouard Dhorme, *Mélanges Louis Massignon* (Damascus: French Institute of Damascus, 1957). See also "The Impact of the Arabic Language on the Visual Arts of Islam" in *Mirror of the Intellect* (Albany, N.Y: SUNY, 1987).

[3] The term "Mohammedan", or better "Mohammedian", does have a role, and means simply "of Mohammed" or "pertaining to Mohammed".

Schuon has pointed out, the role of Mohammed in Islam is in some ways analogous to that of the Virgin Mary in Christianity.[4] The annunciation to Mary, like the revelation to Mohammed, came through the Archangel Gabriel. Mary, a virgin, produced a Son, while Mohammed, an "unlettered" man (*ummī*), produced a Book. Mohammed's "illiteracy", like Mary's virginity, is of profound metaphysical and spiritual significance.

Though Mohammed is viewed simply as a man, he is no ordinary man. Muslims speak of him as a "jewel amongst stones", rather as Christians say of Mary: *benedicta tu in mulieribus* ("blessed art thou amongst women").

At another level, of course, there is an obvious analogy between Mohammed and Christ, as each is the founder and "revealer" of the respective religion. And, very characteristically, Mohammed's role as revealer and legislator is a strongly masculine one.

*
* *

When one speaks of the "Semitic monotheisms" (Judaism, Christianity, Islam), one is contrasting them, as already mentioned, with the "Aryan mythologies", such as Hinduism and Buddhism. Following its revelation to Mohammed, Islam rapidly spread to become the religion of the majority of the Arabs. Both Jews and Arabs, as Semitic peoples, belong to the posterity of Abraham, but whereas the Jews trace their descent from Isaac,[5] the son of Abraham and Sarah, the Arabs (including Mohammed)

---

[4] See "Christianity and Islam" in Frithjof Schuon, *The Transcendent Unity of Religions* (Wheaton, IL: Quest, 1984).

[5] Isaac's son Jacob could be said to be the first Jew.

are descended from Ishmael, the son of Abraham and Hagar. In the book of Genesis (17:20), God speaks to Abraham of his first-born, Ishmael, and says: "Behold I have blessed him, . . . and will make of him a great nation". For Islam, Ishmael plays a cardinal and prophetic role. The Kaaba at Mecca was built by Abraham and Ishmael.

As for Christianity, it was the "Gentile" (or Aryan) Europeans who were destined to embrace it and thereby to become spiritually "Semiticized"—though never entirely losing a certain Aryan cast of mind deriving from classical antiquity and molded also by their Indo-European languages. A number of other Aryan peoples, such as the Persians and many Indians, were spiritually Semiticized by their conversion to the religion of the Arab Prophet. In India, for example, the spiritual and psychological difference between the Aryan Hindus and the spiritually Semiticized Muslims (even though they both belong to the same sub-branch of the Aryan race) is marked.

*
* *

In the next chapter the point will be made that, contrary to the view of some orientalists, Sufism is in principle entirely orthodox. The concept of orthodoxy in general is one which, in our day, is far from being properly understood. It can be approached from two directions: firstly, it represents conformity to the religion as it was revealed; secondly, it represents conformity to truth as such. The two senses do not in principle conflict, as the revelation is itself an expression of the truth (albeit an expression destined to meet the needs and circumstances of a given time and place) and orthodoxy is, as it were, the principle of truth running through the myths, symbols, and dogmas which are the very language of revelation.

Heresy, likewise, can be viewed, either as a departure from the religion as revealed, or else as a departure from truth pure and simple. Seen in this way, the "dogmas" of a religion are not the intellectual prisons that they are often assumed to be, but doorways which, when fully penetrated spiritually, open onto a literally unlimited intellectual freedom.

Another way of looking at it is this: even in the circumstances of today, many people still preserve the notion of "moral purity" and lay high value on it. Orthodoxy is "doctrinal purity", purity in the realm of knowledge. As such, it clearly is of primary importance. Moreover, it is an indispensable condition for any inter-religious dialogue. The reason for this has been well explained by Bernard Kelly:

> Confusion is inevitable whenever cultures based on profoundly different spiritual traditions intermingle without rigid safeguards to preserve their purity. The crusader with the cross emblazoned on his breast, the loincloth and spinning wheel of Mahatma Gandhi when he visited Europe, are images of the kind of precaution that is reasonable when traveling in a spiritually alien territory. The modern traveler in his collar and tie and business suit is safeguarded by that costume against any lack of seriousness in discussing finance. Of more important safeguards he knows nothing. The complete secularism of the modern western world, and wherever its influence has spread, has opened the floodgates to a confusion which sweeps away the contours of the spirit. Traditional norms provide the criteria of culture and civilization. Traditional orthodoxy

is thus the prerequisite of any discourse at all between the traditions themselves.[6]

*
* *

As has already been mentioned, the source of the Islamic religion is the Koran, which was revealed to the Prophet Mohammed. A second source of Muslim doctrine is the *Sunna* (the practice or the wont of the Prophet). The *Sunna* includes not only the customs and usages, but also the Sayings (or "Traditions") of Mohammed (*ahādīth*, sing. *hadīth*). The *ahādīth* are a rich source of Muslim teaching. A particularly important type of *hadīth* is the *hadīth qudsī* in which God Himself speaks through the mouth of the Prophet. Such sayings, although of Divine inspiration, are distinct from the Koranic revelation.

The *Sunna* constitutes a norm for the whole of the Islamic world. Love of the Prophet (who is usually referred to as the "Messenger of God", *Rasūlu 'Llāh*) is much cultivated in Islam, and classically takes the form of conformity to his *Sunna* ("Custom" or "Wont").

The central Message (*risāla*) of Islam is the declaration of faith (*shahāda*): "There is no god but God; Mohammed is the Messenger of God" (*Lā ilāha illā 'Llāh; Muhammadun Rasūlu 'Llāh*). All Muslim doctrine and all Sufi doctrine derive from the *shahāda*.

The Islamic Law or *sharī'a* is characterized by the "Five Pillars (*arkān*) of Islam". These are faith, prayer, fasting, almsgiving, and pilgrimage. Faith (*īmān*) is assent to the *shahāda*. Prayer (*salāt*) is the canonical prayer that is observed five times daily (at dawn, noon, afternoon, sunset, and night). Fasting (*saum*) is the abstention from

---

[6]   *Dominican Studies*, Vol. 7, 1954, p. 256.

food and drink from dawn to sunset observed during the month of Ramadan. Almsgiving (*zakāt*) is the giving of one's goods for charitable purposes ("for widows and orphans"). Pilgrimage (*hajj*) is the pilgrimage to the Kaaba at Mecca which a Muslim should make, if possible, at least once in his lifetime. As we shall see in Chapter 3, Sufism adds to the literal meaning of each of the Five Pillars a metaphysical and spiritual interpretation.

In addition to the Five Pillars of Islam, one should also mention the well-known Muslim prohibition of wine and pork. Wine is a "good thing" in itself, as is proved by the fact that it is promised to the faithful in Paradise, and also by the positive use which many Sufis have made of the imagery of wine and drunkenness to symbolize mystical states.[7] In its negative aspect, however, it is the symbol of confusion and error. Pork is the symbol of uncleanness or sin. In the Semitic perspective it has no positive symbolism, although it should be noted that, according to Guénon, the wild boar (which is a different species) is not covered by the prohibition. Gambling and usury are also forbidden by Islamic law. An interesting sidelight on Islamic attitudes is provided by the fact that it is forbidden for men to wear gold or silk. These two precious substances are reserved for the use of women.

Another well known Islamic concept is that of the "holy war" (*jihād*). Outwardly, this refers to the defense of the Islamic community. Inwardly or spiritually, it refers to the unseen warfare against the ego. Mohammed indicated the relationship of these two aspects of the holy war when, following a battle, he remarked to his companions: "We are returning from the lesser holy war

---

[7] Likewise wine appears at the center of Christian worship as the "blood of Christ".

(against our outward enemies), to the greater holy war (against ourselves)!" Alas, in modern times, the "Islamic" terrorists willfully reject this *hadīth* and abusively invoke the concept of *jihād* as a justification for their diabolic activities.

Islam accepts, and incorporates into itself, all antecedent prophets of Abrahamic lineage, up to and including Jesus and Mary.[8] There are more references in the Koran to the Virgin Mary (*Sayyidatnā Maryam*, "Our Lady Mary") than in the New Testament. One of its chapters is even named after her. As for Jesus (*Sayyidnā 'Īsā*, "Our Lord Jesus"), he is often called the "Seal of Sanctity" (*khātim al-wilāya*). The term "Seal of Prophecy" (*khātim an-nubuwwa*) is given to Mohammed. Jesus and Mary play a certain inward role in the spiritual economy of Sufism. This is particularly apparent in the lives and works of such great Sufis as Muhyi 'd-Dīn ibn 'Arabī and Mansūr al-Hallāj.

*
* *

The only important "division" within Islam is that between Sunnīs and Shī'is. Orthodox (Sunnī) Islam recognizes that the immediate successors (*khalīfas*) to the Prophet Mohammed, as heads of the Islamic community, are the four Caliphs, Abu Bakr, Omar, Othman and Ali. The establishment and subsequent development of Islam as a world religion rests on the pattern set by these four

---

[8] An implicit recognition of the Prophets of the non-Semitic religions is to be found in the Koranic verse: "Verily We have sent Messengers before thee (Mohammed). About some of them We have told thee, and *about some of them We have not told thee*" (*Sūra* "The Believer", 40:78). The Koran also says: "For every community there is a Messenger" (*Sūra* "Jonah", 10:47).

holy patriarchs. Shī'ism, on the contrary, rejects the first three Caliphs and regards the fourth Caliph Ali as the only legitimate immediate successor to the Prophet, the chief reason being that Ali was of the "family of the Prophet", since he was the latter's son-in-law.

The name Shī'a (the general term for Shī'is) comes from *shī'atu 'Alī*, "the party of Ali". Though "schismatical" from the Sunnī point of view, Shī'ism retains most of the orthodox doctrines and practices of Islam—apart, of course, from the major matter of rejecting the first three Caliphs. By diverging in this way from Sunnī Islam, Shī'ism has developed a characteristic religious climate of its own—one which can be witnessed in Persia (where Shī'is predominate) and in a number of other areas where Shī'i communities are to be found. The great Sufi poets of Persia, however, such as Jalāl ad-Dīn Rūmī and Omar Khayyam were Sunnīs.[9]

*
* *

From the time of the Crusades many Christians have considered the Islamic world, bordering as it does on Christendom, to be a threat and rival to the latter. And yet Islam's record towards Christianity is a good one, and its age-old tolerance of Christian and Jewish communities ("People of the Book", *ahl al-kitāb*) living in its midst is well known. Islam's attitude to Christianity has its root in the Koran. One typical verse says: "You will find that the best friends of believers [i.e. Muslims] are those who say: 'We are Christians.' This is because there are priests and

[9] For a penetrating evaluation of the Shī'a schism, see "Images of Islam" in Frithjof Schuon, *Christianity/Islam: Perspectives on Esoteric Ecumenism* (Bloomington, IN: World Wisdom, 2008).

monks amongst them, and because they are not proud" (*Sūra* "The Table", 5:82).

A modern testimony regarding one part of the Muslim world comes from a Catholic missionary: "One can safely say . . . that in Africa's Moslem millions there is a great fund of sincere religious sentiment and of goodwill towards non-Moslems."[10] The late Sir Abubakar Tafewa Balewa of Nigeria, on receiving a message of blessing from Pope Pius XII, kept the Bishops who presented it to him waiting while he read and re-read the message, with tears flowing from his eyes.

Many of the Scholastic philosophers knew and valued the works of Islamic theologians. Dante used Islamic sources in the *Divine Comedy*. In more modern times, Pope Pius XI in dispatching his Apostolic Delegate to Libya, said to him: "Do not think you are going amongst infidels. Muslims attain to Salvation. The ways of God are infinite."[11] Pope Pius XII remarked how consoling it was to know that, all over the world, there were millions of people who, five times a day, bow down before God. The Catholic Bishops of Nigeria, in the concluding words of their joint Pastoral Letter of 1960, afforded a good example of a just Christian attitude towards Islam: "We express sentiments of fraternal love towards our Muslim fellow-citizens. . . . We appreciate their deep spirit of prayer and fasting. . . . We are united against tendencies towards materialism and secularism."[12]

---

[10] Fr. Patrick O'Connor, *Catholic Herald* (London), 9 January 1959.

[11] *L'Ultima*, Florence, VIII, 1954.

[12] *Catholic Herald* (London), 21 October 1960.

*
* *

It cannot be said too often that the religion of Islam stems entirely from the Koran. One of its translators, Marmaduke Pickthall, called it "that inimitable symphony, the very sounds of which move men to tears and ecstasy". In order to let the reader taste a little of the flavor of the Koran as directly as possible, this chapter will end with two characteristic passages, firstly in the original Arabic, and then in English translation.

Inna'l-muslimīna wa'l-muslimāti,
wa'l-mu'minīna wa'l-mu'mināti,
wa'l-qānitīna wa'l-qānitāti,
wa'sādiqīna wa'sādiqāti,
wa's-sābirīna wa's-sābirāti,
wa'l-khāshi'īna wa'l-khāshi'āti,
wa'l-mutasaddiqīna wa'l-mutasaddiqāti,
wa's-sā'imina wa's-sā'imāti,
wa'l-hāfizīna furūja-hum wa'l-hāfizāti,
wa'dh-dhākirīna 'Llāha kathīran wa 'dh-dhākirāti,
ā' adda 'Llāhu la-hum maghfiratan wa ajran 'azīman.

Sūrat al-Ahzāb, 33:35

Verily men who submit [to God] and women who submit,
and men who believe and women who believe,
and men who are devout and women who are devout,
and men who speak the truth and women who speak the truth,
and men who are patient and women who are patient,
and men who are humble and women who are humble,
and men who give alms and women who give alms,
and men who fast and women who fast,
and men who guard their modesty and women who guard,

and men who remember God much and women who
  remember,
God has prepared for them forgiveness and a vast reward.
Sūra "The Confederates", 33:35

Wa 'd-duhā,
wa 'l-laili idhā sajā,
mā wadda'a-ka rabbu-ka wa mā qalā,
wa la 'l-akhiratu khairun la-ka min al-ūlā,
wa la-saufa yu'tī-ka rabbu-ka fa-tardā
a lam yajid-ka yatīman fa-awā?
Wa wajada-ka dallan, fa-hadā?
Wa wajada-ka 'ā'ilan- fa aghnā?
Fa-ammā 'l-yatīma fa-lā taqhar,
wa ammā 's-sā'ila fa-lā tanhar,
wa ammā bi ni'mati rabbi-ka fa-haddith.
Sūrat ad-Duhā, 93:1-11

By the brightness of day,
and by the night when it covereth,
thy Lord hath not forsaken thee nor doth He hate thee,
and verily the next world will be better for thee than this
  one,
and verily thy Lord will give unto thee so that thou wilt
  be content.
Did He not find thee an orphan and protect thee?
Did He not find thee wandering and direct thee?
Did He not find thee destitute and enrich thee?
Therefore the orphan oppress not,
therefore the beggar turn not away,
therefore of the bounty of Thy Lord be thy discourse.
Sūra "The Brightness of Day", 93:1-11

CHAPTER 2

ISLAMIC ESOTERISM (*Haqīqa*)

This chapter will be concerned chiefly with the doctrinal side of the *haqīqa*—the name given to the "inner Truth" or "inner Reality" that is at the heart of the Islamic revelation. The *sharī'a* (outward law) is in fact the vehicle or expression of the *haqīqa*, and this is why Sufis always recognize the outward law. This represents a paradox for those who, for various reasons, consider Sufism to be unorthodox, and a departure, precisely, from the orthodox *sharī'a*.

The explanation is that Sufism, while outwardly conforming, is inwardly free. The *sharī'a* is the doorway that opens on to freedom, the "strait path that leadeth unto life". For the Sufi the "doorway" is not an end in itself. Nevertheless, it remains venerable, and Christian doctrine, as expressed by Saint Paul, puts a much more extreme edge on the matter when it contrasts "the letter that killeth" and "the spirit that giveth life" (2 Cor. 3:6).

It would have been impossible, however, for this inward freedom of Sufism never to have shown itself in a form which appeared to conflict with Islamic orthodoxy. There is the famous case of Al-Hallāj who, having in mind the doctrine of Unity (and above all having himself "realized" man's essential identity with the Divine Principle and so transcended the distinction between "servant" and "Lord"), declared: "I am the Truth" (*anā 'l-Haqq*)—a declaration which earned him martyrdom at the hands of the "exoteric" authorities. In Christianity, the case of Meister Eckhart was analogous.

A freedom which is total will always scandalize those who see no further than the outward limits, and there is even, objectively, from a certain point of view at least, a relationship of opposition between the "inwardly supra-formal" and the "outwardly formal". Meister Eckhart has said: "If thou wouldst reach the kernel, thou must break the shell."

The total freedom in respect of outward forms enjoyed by Sufis of a high degree of spiritual realization does not always lead to martyrdom, however, but sometimes to the most audacious *jeux d'esprit*. What a subtlety of interrelationships is betokened in the following story. The voice of God spoke to the Sufi Abū 'l-Hasan al-Kharraqānī,[1] saying: "Shall I tell the people of thy 'state' [i.e. his 'spiritual drunkenness' or high degree of spiritual realization involving independence of outward forms], so that [being scandalized] they will stone thee?' Abū 'l-Hasan's state was such that he immediately answered back: 'Shall I tell the people of Thine infinite Mercy, so that they will never again bow down to Thee in prayer?'"[2]

---

[1] A Persian of the eleventh century.

[2] Such daring is not limited to Islam. The stage-coach in which Saint Teresa of Ávila was traveling ran into a ditch. As she was extricating herself with some difficulty, she heard a voice saying: "Knowest thou not Teresa, that this is how I treat my friends?" She did not hesitate to answer back: "Then it is small wonder that Thou hast so few of them!"

Therein lies hidden the key to the relationship between exoterism and esoterism!

In summary, let it be said that Sufism cannot be other than orthodox, and this for two reasons: firstly, being the "inward" dimension of the "outward" dogma, it cannot repudiate the latter, though it "frees" itself from the formal constraints of the dogma "from within". Secondly—and this is a point worth stressing—the doctrines and practices of Sufism, as Louis Massignon and other orientalists have amply demonstrated, are entirely derivable from the Koran alone, the Koran being the very basis of Islamic orthodoxy.

This latter fact specifically refutes the allegation that Sufism developed chiefly as a result of influences from extraneous sources such as Neoplatonism, Christianity, or Hinduism. Sufism has sometimes borrowed formulations deriving from Neoplatonic and other spiritual doctrines which coincide with its own view of reality, but this has always been for convenience of expression, and does not constitute any syncretism.

*
* *

The central doctrine of Sufism is *wahdat*[3] *al-wujūd*, which is variously translated as "the oneness of being" or "the Unicity of Existence". This doctrine is derived directly from the *shahāda*, which is understood not only as "there is no god but God" but also as "there is no reality except Reality". One of the Names of God, indeed, is *al-Haqq*, which means "Reality" or "Truth".

---

[3] *Wāhid* ("one") means "one and only" (God has no partners); *ahad* ("one") means "one and undivided" (God has no parts). The noun *wahdat* means "one-and-onliness" or "unicity".

The Sufis teach that the relative has no reality other than in the Absolute, and the finite has no reality other than in the Infinite. In Islam, man has access to the Absolute and the Infinite through the Koran, which is the revelation of God to the world, and also through the Prophet who, within the world itself, is God's very reflection. The content of the Koran, like the message of the Prophet, is essentially *lā ilāha illā 'Llāh, Muhammadun Rasūlu 'Llāh.* In these two revealed and sacred clauses of the *shahāda*, man has access, on the one hand, to the Divine Immutability and, on the other, to the "Mohammedian" or Prophetic Norm.

Muslims have been called "the people of *lā ilāha illā 'Llāh*", and Sufis draw the full spiritual consequences from this their most precious possession. In and through the *shahāda* (with its dual reference to the Divinity and the Prophet), the imperfect is overwhelmed by the Perfect (the "Mohammedian" Norm) and the impermanent is extinguished by the Permanent (God Himself). "Say: Truth has come and falsehood has vanished away. Verily falsehood is ever bound to vanish" (*Sūra* "The Children of Israel", 17:81).

There is no "duality" in the *shahāda*, however. The second clause, referring to the Prophet, is implicitly contained in the first. Frithjof Schuon has indicated how it logically derives from the word *illā*, "except".[4] Nevertheless, the Prophet's role is indispensable for man, as it is only through the Prophet, God's representative, that man may come to God Himself. The Prophet is the personification of the "Word of God" (*Logos*), and it is only through the Logos that man can come to God.

---

[4] See *Understanding Islam* (Bloomington, IN: World Wisdom, 2011), pp. 125-126.

Nor is there any multiplicity in the first clause of the *shahāda*. It can be reduced to one word: *Allāh*, for, precisely, "there is no god but God".

The role of the Logos can be seen in the following diagram:

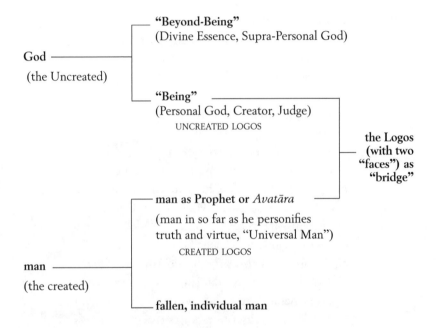

The spiritualities or mysticisms of all of the great religions teach that it is by uniting himself (in prayer and sacrament) with the "created Logos", that man attains to union with God.

Though we are dealing here only with doctrine (and not with "spiritual realization", which is the subject of the next chapter, "The Mystical Path"), it can be seen at once that Sufi doctrine is invariably "operative". That is to say, it is not merely theory, but a path (*tarīqa*) to be followed, as well as a tangible blessing (*baraka*) which acts as a viaticum.

Titus Burckhardt sums up the essential features of Sufism as follows:

> Possessing as it does the dual aspects of wisdom and the love of God, Sufism finds its expression not only in the mental forms of metaphysics but also in poetry and the visual arts, and, as its essence is communicated most directly in symbols and analogies, it can speak without hindrance not only to learned believers, but also to the simple man of the people: the craftsman and the Bedouin; in fact, it may often be received more easily by the unlearned than by the learned.
>
> Though Islamic mysticism, as it persists . . . down to the present day, may be compared in many respects with Christian mysticism—and in other respects with Hindu and Far-Eastern mysticism—it is nevertheless founded entirely on the religious form specific to Islam. Its point of departure is *Tauhīd*, the doctrine of Divine Unity. If Islamic law demands as the first duty of every believer, that he "witness" the Unity of God, Islamic mysticism requires that this witness (*shahāda*) should not merely be a form of lip service, nor even a mental assent, but that it should be, beyond all reflections and sentiments, a total and immediate act of witness (*shahāda*); "witness" such as this means nothing other than the knowledge of God.
>
> God can only be known, however, when the human ego, which instinctively regards itself as a self-sufficient center—a kind of "divinity" in addition to the Divinity—is extinguished before the infinitude of God, in accordance with the

words: "There is no divinity but God". This does not mean that the immortal essence of the soul has to be annihilated; what must be dissolved is that mental morass, compounded of ego-determined passions and imaginings, the constant tendency of which is to restrict consciousness to the level of ephemeral appearances. When this "veil" of selfishness is lifted from the Spirit which is hidden underneath—the Spirit which sees through to the essences of things—then for the first time things are seen as they really are. God is seen in His all-embracing Presence, and the creature as a pure possibility contained in the Divine Being.

The organ by means of which man takes cognizance of the presence of God is, according to Sufi teaching, not the brain but the heart. As with the Christian Fathers, the heart is the seat, not of the sentiments, but of the Intellect or Spirit (*ar-Rūh*), which penetrates to Reality and transcends mental forms.

Deflected from the true center of his being, which has its roots in the Eternal, the consciousness of the average man is as if imprisoned in a kind of dream or state of forgetfulness (*ghafla*). This is why man must be "reminded" (of That which he has "forgotten"), and this is the reason for what is known as *dhikr*, which the Sufi must practice in a large variety of ways, and which means "recollection" or "mindfulness" as well as "contemplation" and "invocation". The practice of *dhikr* is directly analogous to the "prayer of the heart" of the Hesychasts of Eastern Christianity.

The goal of the mystical path is the transcending

of the ego, and this path cannot be embarked upon without grace (*taufīq*).[5]

Mention of *ar-Rūh* calls for the following remarks. In traditional metaphysics "intellectual" or "spiritual" are the adjectives pertaining to the third element in the ternary constituting the human being which, in scholastic terms, is: *corpus* (body), *anima* (soul), and *Spiritus vel Intellectus* (Spirit or Intellect). The middle term "soul" comprises, amongst other things, the mind or reason, the adjectives pertaining to which are, of course, "mental" or "rational". In modern parlance, however, the term "intellectual" is often wrongly used as a synonym for these, in spite of the fact that it properly pertains only to "Intellect" (or "Spirit"). "Intellectual" and "spiritual" are more or less equivalent terms, the first putting the emphasis on the "doctrinal" aspect and the second on the "methodic" or "realizational" aspect. Whereas body and soul are purely human and belong to the "individual" domain, the Spirit or Intellect is "universal" and transcends the human state as such. As already indicated, the Latin *Spiritus vel Intellectus* ("Spirit or Intellect") corresponds to the Arabic *Rūh*. *Anima* ("soul") corresponds to the Arabic *nafs*. See the following table:

English	Latin	Greek	Arabic
Spirit (Intellect)	*Spiritus (Intellectus)*	*Pneuma (Nous)*	*Rūh ('Aql)*
soul	*anima*	*psyche*	*nafs*
body	*corpus*	*soma*	*jism*

---

[5] *Fez: City of Islam* (Cambridge, UK: Islamic Texts Society, 1992), pp. 129-130.

The element "soul" can be said to contain all the human faculties, as follows:

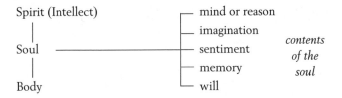

Spirit (Intellect)
|
Soul —————————
|
Body

— mind or reason
— imagination
— sentiment
— memory
— will

contents of the soul

In view of the importance of the element "will" in morality and spirituality, it can also be classified separately from the other faculties, and here one speaks of the ternary: "intelligence-will-soul" or "intelligence-will-sentiment" or "intelligence-will-character".

The most all-inclusive metaphysical doctrine in Islam is the "Five Levels of Reality" or the "Five Divine Presences" (*al-Hadarāt al-ilāhīya al-khams*). In Persia, it was expounded by 'Azīz-i Nasafī. It is summarized in the following table in Arabic and with English explanations:

	Arabic	English
1	*Hāhūt*	Beyond-Being (Divine Essence)
2	*Lāhūt*	Being (God as Creator, Helper, Judge)
3	*Jabarūt*	Spirit, Intellect, Heaven, Angelic World
4	*malakūt*	soul
5	*nāsūt*	body

All the various relationships deriving from this doctrine are elaborated in greater detail in the following comprehensive table:

			Level						
The Divine			**(1) BEYOND-BEING** (the Divine Essence, the Supra-Personal God)		ABSOLUTE	ĀTMĀ	DIVINE	HEAVEN	IMMORTAL
The Unmanifest The Uncreated The Metacosmic			**(2) BEING** (the Personal God, Creator, Judge; Divine Qualities)	UNCREATED LOGOS	RELATIVE	MĀYĀ			
EXISTENCE	Universal or Supra-formal Manifestation		**(3) Spirit, Intellect** (Spiritual, Intellectual, or Angelic realm)	CREATED LOGOS			HUMAN		
The Manifest The Created The Cosmic	individual or formal manifestation	subtle	**(4) soul** (animic or psychic realm)					EARTH	
		gross	**(5) body** (corporeal realm)						MORTAL

Right-hand vertical column groupings: ABSOLUTE / RELATIVE; ĀTMĀ / MĀYĀ; DIVINE / HUMAN; HEAVEN / EARTH; IMMORTAL / MORTAL; UNCREATED LOGOS / CREATED LOGOS.

The nature and function of the Intellect is succinctly evoked in the words of Dante (*Paradiso*, IV:124-125):

> *Io veggio ben, che giammai non so sazia*
> *Nostro intelletto se il ver non lo illustra.*
> Now do I see that never will our Intellect be sated,
> Unless the Truth do shine upon it.

In Christianity, doctrines analogous to those of Sufism are to be found, in the Western Church, in the writings of Meister Eckhart, Angelus Silesius and certain others, and, in the Eastern Church, in the great exponents of apophatic and antinomian theology such as Saint Gregory Palamas, whose doctrine of the Divine Essence and the Divine Energies corresponds closely to the Sufi doctrine regarding *Dhāt* ("Essence") and *Sifāt* ("Qualities").

An essential difference between the two religions, however, is that whereas Islam possesses an exoteric domain—*sharī'a* or (outward) Law—and an esoteric domain—*haqīqa* or (inward) Truth—no such division exists in Christianity. According to a certain Islamic point of view, Christianity is a pure *haqīqa* (esoterism), which came into the world without a complementary exoteric component of its own. This view receives confirmation in Christ's own words: *regnum meum non est de hoc mundo* ("My Kingdom is not of this world"). Seen from this angle, certain ambiguities discernible in Christianity derive from the fact that, historically, this esoterism had to undergo an exoteric application, in an effort, so to speak, to make good the missing exoterism. This *de facto* extension of the Christian revelation (a *haqīqa*, in Islamic terminology) to the outward domain could not, of course, in any way alter the original nature of the Christian dogmas and sacraments, which continue to be "esoteric" formulations and "initiatic" rites respectively.[6]

As far as the spiritualities of the two religions are concerned, Christian mysticism tends by and large to be characterized by the "Way of Love" (*mahabba*, in Islamic terminology),[7] whereas Islamic mysticism (i.e. Sufism) comprises both the "Way of Knowledge" (*ma'rifa*) and the "Way of Love" (*mahabba*).[8] This is one reason why the more "gnostic" or "jnanic" formulations of Islamic mysticism tend to strike a foreign note to those familiar only with the Christian forms of spirituality.[9]

This distinction between Christianity and Islam (between "Love" and "Knowledge") also shows itself in the answers given by the two religions to the question: why was the world created? In Christianity it is customary to say that God created the world "out of love". While this statement would not be regarded as untrue in Islam either,

---

[6] See "Mystères Christiques" by Frithjof Schuon in *Études Traditionnelles*, Paris, July-August 1948.

[7] Some of those who, exceptionally, represent the "Way of Knowledge" in Christianity have just been mentioned.

[8] *Ma'rifa* and *mahabba* correspond respectively to the *jñāna-mārga* and the *bhakti-mārga* of the Hindus.

[9] It is interesting to note in this connection that it is the very existence, in Islam, of an exoterism in the full sense of the word, that occasionally causes Christians to see something "earthy" (not "worldly") in some of the outward manifestations of Islam. Contrariwise, the exclusively esoteric nature of the Christian revelation tempts Muslims to regard Christians (who by and large fail to live up to the high spiritual demands of their "esoterism") as hypocrites! In recent times, this contrast between Islamic "exoterism" and Christian "spirituality" has caused many in the Western public to believe that this is positive proof that Christianity is the superior religion!

a haunting and beautiful reference (more characteristic of the Islamic perspective) to the mystery of existence, is provided in the *hadīth qudsī*: "I was a hidden treasure, and I wished to be *known*, so I created the world."

*

* *

The doctrine of the "oneness of being" has led some to think that Sufi doctrine is a form of "pantheism". This is entirely misleading, as the term pantheism is normally used to designate certain European philosophic concepts of recent centuries that have nothing to do with any traditional doctrines, whether scholastic or mystical. Pantheism (the belief, for example, that God is the sum total of all things) implies a "substantial" identity between the Principle and manifestation, or between the Creator and the created. This is foreign to all "traditional" doctrine, which insists on the gulf between the Absolute and the relative, or the Infinite and the finite, going so far as to call the first element in each case "Real" and the second (relatively) "unreal", ephemeral.[10]

There is, however, an "essential" (not "substantial") identity between the created and the Creator, whence, precisely, the "relative reality" of the world in which we live. Once again Sufi doctrine derives from the *shahāda*: "there is no reality except Reality". Here the reference is to the essential identity of all that is, and to the nothingness of that which is not. The Sufi doctrine of *wahdat al-wujūd* is, in fact, the equivalent of the Vedantic *advaita*, which some have called "monism", but which is perhaps more accurately translated as "non-duality".

[10] Cf. the saying of Christ: "Heaven and earth shall pass away, but My words will not pass away" (Matt. 24:35).

The point is that the world does not have a different principle from God. As the Hindus have put it, "the world *is* God (i.e. as far as its essential principle is concerned), but God is not the world". This second proposition is, in fact, the basic error of latter-day European pantheistic trends, be these poetic or philosophic. Sufism, on the contrary, is an expression of traditional doctrine on this matter.

*
* *

It might be asked: what is Sufism's attitude towards the modern world and the belief in "progress". It is known that the Hindus teach that we are living in the latter period of the "Dark Age" (*kali-yuga*),[11] in which men turn from the "total" to the fragmentary, from the profound to the superficial, and from the spiritual to the material— at an ever-accelerating pace, moreover, until mankind reaches the final, cataclysmic end. Similar doctrines and prophecies are to be found in Buddhism, Christianity, and the religion of the North American Indians.

The Islamic view is given tersely in a Tradition (*hadīth*) of the Prophet: "No time cometh upon you but is followed by a worse!" This sets the tone for the characteristic "conservatism" of Sufism which, as far as the outward world is concerned, seeks above all to protect sacred—and salvific—forms from the erosions of time and ever-increasing indifference. Those living in the latter times enjoy certain compensations, however. In the Christian parable of the laborers in the vineyard, those who

---

[11] The Hindu doctrine of the four *Yugas* (*Satya, Treta, Dvapara,* and *Kali*) corresponds to the Greco-Roman doctrine of the Four Ages, spoken of by Hesiod and Ovid, namely Golden, Silver, Bronze, and Iron.

worked only for the last period before "sunset", received the same wage as those who had worked throughout the whole day. And the Prophet of Islam declared that in the earliest days he who omitted a tenth of the Law would be damned, whereas in the latter days he who accomplishes a tenth of the Law will be saved. In the "Dark Age", which corresponds to the Greco-Roman "Iron Age", there can be no greater message of hope and encouragement for exoterist and esoterist alike.

*
*　*

In the Introduction reference was made to the symbolism of the radii of a circle: the nearer they are to the center, the nearer they are to each other, and in the center itself the radii unite. It is naturally the esoteric doctrines—the doctrines of "love" and "gnosis" (or "knowledge")—of the various religions that are closest to one another. If one compares social customs and laws of inheritance, one need not expect to find identity; but the nearer one gets to the "center"—to the doctrines concerning the glory of God, the indigence of man, the ways of salvation—the nearer one gets to unanimity. In India, the "social" differences between Islam and Hinduism could scarcely be greater, yet Prince Dara Shikoh, son of the Emperor Shah Jahan and Mumtaz Mahal, declared: "The science of Vedanta and the science of Sufism are one."[12]

There is surely no more beautiful testimony to the transcendent unity of the religions than the haunting declaration of one of the great Islamic masters of "gnosis", ash-Shaikh al-Akbar Muhyi 'd-Dīn ibn ʿArabī, who

---

[12] Sikhism, for its part, seems to have been a sort of fusion of Hindu *bhakti* and Muslim *mahabba*.

flourished in Andalusia at the end of the twelfth and the beginning of the thirteenth century: "My heart has become capable of every form: it is a pasture for gazelles, a cloister for Christian monks, a temple for idols, the Kaaba of the pilgrim, the tablets of the Torah, and the Book of the Koran. I practice the religion of Love. In whatsoever directions its caravans advance, the religion of Love shall be my religion and my faith."[13]

---

[13] Regarding Ibn 'Arabī's use of the expression "the religion of Love", Frithjof Schuon comments as follows: "Here it is not a question of *mahabba* in the psychological or methodological sense, but of a truth that is lived, and of 'divine attraction'. Here 'love' is contrasted with 'forms', which are envisaged as 'cold' and as 'dead'. Saint Paul also says that 'the letter killeth, but the spirit maketh alive'. 'Spirit' and 'love' are here synonymous" (*Understanding Islam*, p. 30n)

Tomb of Muhyi 'd-Dīn ibn 'Arabī, near Damascus, Syria

CHAPTER 3

THE MYSTICAL PATH (*Tarīqa*)

The object of all religion is salvation. Religion is always doctrine with a view to "realization". The doctrine is never mere theory, but always "operative" in intent. Consequently, in religion, doctrine and method, or theory and practice, are indissolubly wed. Doctrine concerns the mind (or, at the highest level, the "intellect" in the Medieval or Eckhartian sense of this term); method (or practice) concerns the will. Religion, to be itself, must always engage both "mind" and "will".

The operative side of religion, in the ordinary sense of this term, manifests itself in two main ways: morality and worship. Morality is self-explanatory: "doing the things which ought to be done and not doing the things which ought not to be done". Worship takes two forms: participation in the public rites of the religion, and the performance of private works of piety, classically summed up under the headings "prayer" and "fasting".[1]

---

[1] This is a general (and not a specifically Islamic) reference to private devotions. It does not refer to the public Islamic rites of *salāt* and *ramadān*.

Religion, then, is concerned with salvation. In order to embark on the path that leads to salvation one must obviously be a member of the religion which teaches it and which, on certain conditions, "guarantees" it. Salvation is ordinarily conceived as being attainable only after death—a rejoining of the saints in paradise. The only difference between spirituality (or mysticism) and religion in the ordinary sense, is that spirituality envisages as its main end the attaining of sanctity (or the embarking on the path that leads to sanctity) even in this life, here and now. All spiritual doctrine, and all spiritual method, are orientated towards this end. This is what the mystical or initiatic path is all about.

To embark on a spiritual or mystical path, a rite of initiation is indispensable. This is the case in all of the religions. The rite of initiation, which may be compared to the planting of a seed, imparts on the disciple a specific spiritual influence which effectuates the beginning (*initium*) of his "new", inward, life. No seed, no life, no growth. No initiation, no rebirth, no sanctification. In Sufism, the aspirant receives the rite of initiation from a Sufi master (*shaikh* or *murshid*) who, in his turn, has received it, at the beginning of his spiritual career, from his sheikh or spiritual master, and so on back to the Prophet himself who, by Divine Grace, initiated the first Sufis.

The name "Sufi" did not exist in the time of the Prophet, but the reality did. The Prophet conferred this rite (and gave the corresponding counsels) to only some of his Companions; they in turn passed it on, and in this way, up to the present day, the rite, in unbroken succession, is still passed on. This chain of initiation is known in Arabic as *silsila*. The various Sufi methods of spiritual realization (to which reference will later be made) cannot validly be practised without the initiation, and the counsel, of a sheikh or spiritual master. To attempt to do so would be to court considerable spiritual danger.

The majority of Muslims are not Sufis, and have not received this rite of initiation. The situation in Christianity is quite different. The Christian rite of initiation is baptism. It is clear that since early times baptism has been routinely administered to infants. In this, Christianity is exceptional, for it is unusual for initiation to be conferred on all, and also at an age which rules out conscious desire on the part of those to be initiated. This state of affairs, however, springs from the historical phenomenon in Christianity earlier referred to, namely the application of an esoterism (*haqīqa*) to the exoteric or social domain, thus causing it to play a role analogous to that of the *sharī'a* in Islam.

Nevertheless, since an esoteric rite applied exoterically remains esoteric in itself, it follows that all Christians are in principle initiates; that is to say, their spiritual status is in principle analogous to that of the Sufis.[2] Certainly a Christian seeking to embark on a spiritual path within Christianity has no need of further initiation. The overwhelming majority of Christians, of course, do not seek to exploit in any full sense the initiation which they indubitably possess. Technically (if not actually) speaking, they are comparable to those Muslims (*mutabarrikūn*)[3] who receive the rite of initiation, not with the intention of following a spiritual path, but for the sake of its "blessing" (*baraka*) and as a reinforcement of their pious efforts faithfully to observe the law of Islam. Christian initiation (baptism) is exploited fully only by the saints. Frithjof

---

[2] It will be recalled that, although strictly speaking, the term Sufi applies only to those who have reached the goal (the saints), it is permissible to extend it to all who have received initiation with a view to traveling along the path.

[3] Cf. *sālikūn*, "travelers" along the spiritual path.

Schuon has referred to this particular difference between Islam and Christianity as follows: "In Islam there is no sanctity other than in esoterism; in Christianity there is no esoterism other than in sanctity."

In Sufism, the aspirant must fulfill two general conditions or requirements. These are an adherence to the religion of Islam and a sincere desire for a spiritual path with a view to a deeper understanding of the outward religion, together with the assimilation of the essential virtues of humility and generosity. It has been said that "Sufism is sincerity (*sidq*)."

*
* *

The central element in Sufism is the spiritual master or sheikh, around whom disciples gather and from whom disciples receive the initiation which, through a long chain (*silsila*), is ultimately derived from the Prophet Mohammed himself. Many generations having occurred between the time of the Prophet and the present day, the *silsilas* are now many and complex, but all of them can be traced back to one or other of those Companions whom the Prophet himself initiated, notably to the Caliphs Abu Bakr and Ali. A demonstration of these "chains of descent" can be found in Martin Lings' book *A Sufi Saint of the Twentieth Century.*[4] The "family tree" of Sufi masters, from the earliest times to the present day, is replete with examples of outstanding holiness. In many instances the names of these saints have been given to those "branches" of the tree over which their particular radiance shines. These branches (Sufi "orders" or "brotherhoods") are known as *turuq* (the plural of *tarīqa* = "path"), and are

---

[4]   London: Allen & Unwin, 1971, pp. 232-233.

indeed so many paths to *haqīqa*, the Inward, Divine Reality, or, in other words, to God Himself.

The first great Sufi order to appear in the form in which *tarīqas* (or *turuq*) are now known was the Qādirī *tarīqa*, which took its name from its illustrious founder, the Sheikh 'Abd al-Qādir al-Jīlānī (1078-1166). This was an off-shoot of the older Junaidī *tarīqa* which stemmed from the great Abū 'l-Qāsim al-Junaid of Baghdad (d. 910). Amongst the next to appear were the Suhrawardī *tarīqa*, whose founder was Shihāb ad-Dīn as-Suhrawardī (1144-1234), and the venerable Shādhilī *tarīqa*, founded by one of the greatest luminaries of Western Islam, the Sheikh Abū 'l-Hasan ash-Shādhilī (1196-1258). Another order to be created about the same period was the Maulāwī *tarīqa* (better known by its Turkish name Mevlevi), so called after the title *Maulānā* or *Mevlana* ("our Lord"), given by his disciples to the founder of the order, Jalāl ad-Dīn Rūmī (1207-1273), author of the *Mathnāwī*, and perhaps the greatest mystical poet of Islam. The most characteristic feature of the Mevlevi order is the famous whirling dance performed by the *fuqarā*[5] as an outward support for their *dhikr* ("invocation" or "prayer of the heart"). This dance is still performed at Konya in Turkey where Rūmī's tomb is located.

In spite of all the differences between them, one cannot refrain from comparing these four venerable Sufi orders (which crystallized in the twelfth and thirteenth centuries and which exist down to the present day) with the three great monastic orders of Western Christendom (which were likewise founded around the same time, and took their names from their founding saints):

---

[5] Plural of *faqīr* ("poor", "poor in spirit"). Members of Sufi orders are known as *fuqara* (or, in the Persian form, "dervishes"). This is how Sufis refer to themselves.

"Indication of the Brotherhoods" (*bayān at-turuq*)
(These words are inscribed on the crescent.)

The Mystical Path (Tarīqa)

NOTE ON THE ILLUSTRATION (Opposite)

At the foot of the trunk is the name *Allāh*. Above this are the names Gabriel and Mohammed. The four large leaves at the top of the trunk bear the names of the first four Caliphs: Abū Bakr, Omar, Othman, 'Alī. The names of the different brotherhoods (*turuq*) are inscribed on the leaves of the tree, but not in any particular order. As explained in the present chapter, each brotherhood is named after its founding saint, through whom, by a chain (*silsila*) of previous spiritual masters, it can trace its descent back either to Ali or Abu Bakr, and thence to the Prophet.

On the five-pointed star (symbol of the Five Pillars of Islam) are the words "The Book [of God] and the Custom or Wont [of the Prophet]" (*Al-Kitāb wa's-Sunna*). For the symbolism of the crescent, see Abū Bakr Sirāj ad-Dīn, *The Book of Certainty* (Cambridge, UK: Islamic Texts Society, 1992).

Majlis and *dhikr* of the Mevlevi dervishes
(from a nineteenth century woodcut)

Benedictines, Dominicans, and Franciscans. Having made the comparison, let one distinguishing mark immediately be mentioned: the Sufi orders do not impose celibacy, though their members may well be committed to exacting fasts, abstinences, and vigils.[6]

The most renowned Sufi order to originate in India—and which did so at about the same time as those mentioned above—is the Chishtī *tarīqa*, founded by Mu'īn ad-Dīn Chishtī (1142-1236), whose tomb at Ajmer is one of the most famous shrines in the subcontinent, and is visited and revered by Hindus and Muslims alike. Another order important throughout the East is the Naqshbandī order, founded in the fourteenth century by Pīr Mohammed Naqshbandī. A widely disseminated order in Western Islam is the Darqāwī, a relatively recent sub-group of the Shādhilī *tarīqa*, having been founded by the Moroccan sheikh Mulay al-'Arabī ad-Darqāwī (c. 1743-1823).

---

[6] Mention of the differences between monks and *fuqarā* recalls the friendship, in mid-twentieth century, between the Bishop of Tripoli (a Franciscan of humble origin) and the Mayor (a Muslim of noble lineage). The Mayor was rich, married, and a leader of men, yet so much did his piety shine through the existential "envelopes" surrounding it, that the Bishop declared that in few other people had he seen the three monastic vows of poverty, chastity, and obedience exemplified to such a high degree. This judgement may strike some as strange, but what the perceptive Bishop had detected was that the Mayor possessed "detachment", and detachment from riches is "poverty", detachment in marriage is "chastity", and detachment when exercising authority is "obedience" to the Source of all authority. Thus outward differences between Sufis and monks do not necessarily preclude that inwardly their essential qualities may be the same. See Duke Alberto Denti di Pirajno, *A Cure for Serpents* (London: Pan Books, 1957), pp. 151-160.

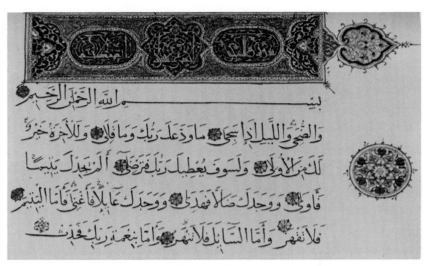

Koran: *Sūra* "The Brightness of Day", 93:1-11 (see p. 22)

The Ninety-Nine Names of God
Top: "To God belong the most beautiful Names; call upon Him by them"
(*Sūra* "The Heights", 7:180) (see pp. 91-92).
Center: "He is God. There is no god but He" (*Sūra* "The Story", 28:70).

I

Fez, Morocco: Karawiyin
Mosque (tenth century)

Granada, Spain:
The Alhambra: The
Courtyard of the Lions
(thirteenth-fourteenth
centuries)

II

Córdoba, Spain: The Great Mosque, the Hall of Prayer (ninth century)

Konya, Turkey: Ince Minara,
Main Doorway (twelfth-thirteenth centuries)

Agra, India: The Taj Mahal
(seventeenth century)

Delhi, India: Jama Masjid "Congregational Mosque" (seventeenth century)

The Mystical Path (Tarīqa)

An illustrious spiritual descendant of Mulay al-'Arabī ad-Darqāwī was the Algerian sheikh Ahmad al-'Alawī (1869-1934), "whose erudition and saintliness", as A.J. Arberry has written, "recall the golden age of the medieval mystics."[7]

It should be mentioned that the founding of an order or brotherhood by an outstanding sheikh does not mean the creation of a new "sect". All the Sufi orders are expressions of Islamic spirituality, and are only differentiated in that each one is "perfumed" by the *baraka* ("blessing") of its original founder, and employs the spiritual methods taught by that particular master. The "whirling" of the Mevlevis and the spiritual retreat (*khalwa*) of the Darqāwīs are examples of particular methods pertaining to a given order.

*

* *

The practice of the religion of Islam involves the believer in the three great categories *islām* (submission to the revealed law), *īmān* (faith in the *shahāda*), and *ihsān* (virtue or sincerity). The following Tradition (*hadīth*) was reported by the Caliph Omar:

> One day when we were with the Messenger of God there came unto us a man whose clothes were of exceeding whiteness and whose hair was of exceeding blackness, nor were there any signs of travel upon him, although none of us had seen him before. He sat down knee unto knee opposite the Prophet, upon whose thighs he placed the palms of his hands, saying: "O Mohammed, tell me what is the surrender unto God (*al-islām*)."

---

[7] *Luzac's Oriental List*, London, October-December 1961.

The Prophet answered: "The surrender is that thou shouldst testify that there is no god but God and that Mohammed is God's Apostle, that thou shouldst perform the prayer, bestow the alms, fast Ramadan, and make, if thou canst, the pilgrimage to the Holy House." He said: "Thou hast spoken truly" and we were amazed that having questioned him he should corroborate him. Then he said: "Tell me what is faith (*īmān*)", and the Prophet answered: "It is that thou shouldst believe in God and His Angels and His Books and His Apostles and the Last Day, and thou shouldst believe that no good or evil cometh but by His Providence." "Thou hast spoken truly," he said, and then: "Tell me what is excellence (*ihsān*)." The Prophet answered: "It is that thou shouldst worship God as if thou sawest Him, for if thou seest Him not, verily He seeth thee". . . . Then the stranger went away, and I stayed there long after he had gone, until the Prophet said to me: "Omar, knowest thou the questioner, who he was?" I said: "God and His Prophet know best, but I know not at all." "It was Gabriel," said the Prophet. "He came to teach you your religion."[8]

The following of a spiritual way (the operative side of Sufism) implies the inner illumination of *islām* and *īmān* by *ihsān*. It necessitates a true vocation, and dedication of a heroic order. The central spiritual method of Sufism, as we shall see presently, is *dhikr* or, more fully, *dhikru 'Llāh* ("invocation" or "the repetition of the Name of God"),

[8] Translated by Martin Lings in *A Sufi Saint of the Twentieth Century* (Cambridge, UK: Islamic Texts Society, 1993), pp. 44-45.

but before aspiring to make use of this, the Sufi must first have a symbolic understanding of the Five Pillars of Islam (faith, prayer, fasting, almsgiving, pilgrimage) and practice them in an "inward" manner. This is indeed an aspect of the Way itself. The Sufi interpretation of faith (*īmān*) has been indicated in the last chapter. As for ritual prayer (*salāt*), the Sufi sees this, not only as an expression of man's "slavehood" (*'ubūdiya*) towards his Lord (*Rabb*), but also as the creature's participation in the song of praise that binds the whole of creation to the Creator. *Salāt* is performed not only by ordinary men, but also by prophets and even angels, and leads them into the invisible channels along which flow the blessings (*salāt*) and the peace (*salām*) of God. Fasting (*saum*) is a reminder of the utter dependence of the "poor" (*fuqarā*) on Him Who is "rich beyond any need of all the worlds" (*ghāniyun 'āni 'l-'ālamīn*). Almsgiving (*zakāt*) reminds the Sufi of his initiatic vow that all his goods and his very life belong only to God, and also that he and his brothers are "members one of another". The pigrimage (*hajj*) to the Kaaba in Mecca is the outward symbol of the inward journey to the "heart" (*qalb*), which is the seat of the Intellect (*'aql*) and is the mysterious center where the Divine Spirit (*ar-Rūh*) touches the human soul.

*
* *

Another important Sufi practice which is, so to speak, preparatory for the *dhikr* (the invocatory prayer which "vehicles" the Sufi's "remembrance" of God) is the recitation of the *wird* or rosary. The *wird* differs slightly from one *tarīqa* to another, but it always comprises essentially the same three formulas. In the first, the *faqīr* asks forgiveness of God. In the second, he asks God to bless the Prophet and give him Peace. The third formula comprises the *shahāda*, the attestation of the Divine Unity. The *wird* is normally recited morning and evening, each formula being repeated a hundred times, for which purpose a chaplet (*tasbīh*) is used. (Sometimes the number of times can be reduced to thirty-three.)

The first formula symbolically represents the Sufi's "movement" from outward to inward, from "existence" to "Being", from the human to the Divine. The second formula is the Sufi's participation in the Mohammedian Norm, which is permeated and sustained, precisely, by the Divine Blessing (*salāt*) and Peace (*salām*). It is a symbolic reintegration of the "fragment" (man) in the Totality (Mohammed), Mohammed being the personification of the total Creation. The Mohammedian Norm is referred to by some Sufis as *al-insān al-kāmil*, "Universal Man". The third formula ("there is no reality other than the Reality") represents the extinction of everything that is not God. The Koran says: "Everything on the earth shall pass away (*fān*); there remaineth (*yabqā*) but he face of thy Lord resplendent with Majesty and Bounty" (*Sūra* "The All-Merciful, 55:26-27).[9] From the foregoing it can be seen that the three formulas of the wird correspond to the three "stages" known in Christian mysticism as: purification, perfection, union. They correspond first and foremost to the three universal aspects of all spirituality: humility, charity, veracity.

*
* *

[9] This verse is the origin of the Sufi concepts of "extinction" (*fanā*) and "permanence" (*baqā*). The "extinction of extinctions" (*fana'u 'l-fanā*) spoken of by some Sufis corresponds to "permanence" (*baqā*). For a Christian parallel, see chap. 2, note 10.

The Sufi spiritual method par excellence is the *dhikr*. This word, often translated as "invocation", has the dual meaning of "remembrance" and "mention". The Koran is replete with injunctions to "remember" God by invoking His Name: "Invoke the Name of thy Lord and devote thyself to Him with utter devotion" (*Sūra* "The Enshrouded One", 73:8). "Remember God with much remembrance" (*Sūra* "The Confederates", 33:41). "Ritual prayer (*salāt*) preserves from uncleanness and grave sin, but verily the remembrance of God is greater" (*wa la-dhikru'Llāhi akbar*) (*Sūra* "The Spider", 29:45). "Verily in the remembrance of God do hearts find rest" (*Sūra* "The Thunder", 13:28). "Remember Me and I shall remember you" (*Sūra* "The Cow", 2:152).

Man finds himself entrapped in manifestation. Manifestation is doomed to impermanence, and this impermanence inevitably entails separation, suffering, and death. All traditional metaphysics teaches that the Principle alone is permanent—and blissful. Once again we are brought back to the message of the *shahāda*: "there is no permanence except in the Permanent", "there is no reality other than the Real". The doctrine of the *dhikr* is that the Divine Name (*Allāh*) directly vehicles the Principle, and when the believer unites himself with the Divine Name in fervent invocation, he inwardly frees himself from manifestation and its concomitant suffering.

Virtual at first, this liberation becomes effective through perseverance and the grace of God *taufīq*). Without the grace of God, the *dhikr* can be a mortal danger. Hence the prohibition to attempt to practice it "methodically" without initiation and the guidance of a sheikh. Any Muslim, however, provided his intention is just, may practice the *dhikr* intermittently and for short periods. In Sufism, on the other hand, the *dhikr* is central to the spiritual method and, in principle, the Sufi seeks to practice it, under the guidance of a spiritual master,

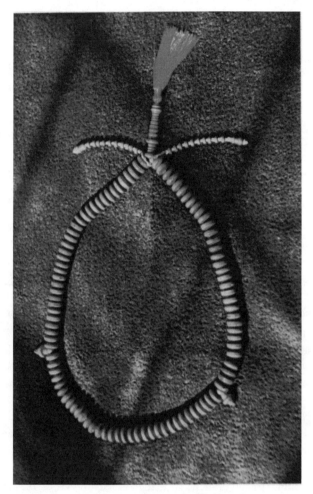

Darqāwī rosary (*tasbih*)

without interruption. The two main supports for the *dhikr* are the *majlis* (session, meeting or gathering of *fuqarā*) and the *khalwa* (spiritual retreat). In most *turuq*, *majālis* (plural of *majlis*) are held at regular intervals under the aegis of the sheikh or his representative (*muqaddam*), and at them the *fuqarā* may make the *dhikr* together for an hour or more. This may be done silently or in the form of a chant, motionlessly or accompanied by a rhythmic swaying which may take the form of a dance.

Sometimes the *dhikr* (and the dance, when peformed) is accompanied by the rhythmic beating of a drum or by music, either vocal or instrumental. *Khalawāt* (plural of *khalwa*) are solitary spiritual retreats for the purpose of invocation. These are made from time to time and may last for as short as several hours or as long as several days. Complementary to these two "formal" supports for the *dhikr* is the frequent silent invocation of the Divine Name at any time of day, in the midst of other activities.

The symbolism of alchemy is sometimes used to describe the practice of the *dhikr*. The soul in its chaotic, unregenerate state is "lead". The philosopher's stone is the Divine Name, in contact with which the "leaden" soul is transmuted into "gold", which is its true nature. This true nature has been lost, but is recovered by the practice of the *dhikr*. The "alchemical work" thus symbolizes the "work of spiritual realization". In either case the essential operation is a "transmutation" of that which is "base" into that which is "noble". The science of the macrocosm (the outward world) thus analogically coincides with the science of the microcosm (the inward world, or soul).

The Sufi doctrine of the *dhikr* coincides with that taught by the nineteenth century Hindu saint Rāmakrishna, who succinctly summed it up in the phrase: "God and His Name are one." In Hinduism the method of constant invocation of the Divine Name (or of a formula containing the Divine Name) is known as *japa*. The Psalms, Gospels, and the Epistles of Saint Paul are full of allusions to the saving power of the Divine Name: "Whoever calls on the Name of the Lord shall be saved." In Eastern Christianity, invocation of the Divine Name (the "prayer without ceasing" enjoined by Saint Paul) takes the form of the "Jesus Prayer",[10] a practice made familiar by the widely disseminated book *Way of a Pilgrim*. In Western Christendom, the revelations made to Sister Consolata, an Italian Capuchin nun, in the earlier part of the twentieth century, revived the Medieval invocation *Jesu-Maria*.[11] Thus do the religions meet, not only in pure metaphysics, but also in pure prayer.

The practice of the *dhikr* goes hand-in-hand with the practice of the virtues. Virtue is seen essentially as self-effacement (*faqr* or *poverty*) and it is said that there can be no *dhikr* without *faqr*. Once again the Arabic language makes apparent an essential identity of content when the same truth is given a different form: only the *faqīr* (the one who is "poor in spirit") may be a *dhākir* (one who invokes God).

The Koran forges the link between *dhikr* and virtue, when it says: "Call upon your Lord humbly and in secret. Lo, He loveth not transgressors. Work not confusion in the earth after the fair ordering thereof, and call on Him in fear and hope. Verily the mercy of God is nigh unto the good" (*Sūra* "The Heights", 7:55-56).

The virtues tend to fall into two groups: the active and the passive. Frithjof Schuon has explained how spiritual "activity" and spiritual "passivity" have their prototypes in two Koranic passages (one about the palm-tree and the other about the *mihrāb* or prayer niche) concerning the Virgin Mary (*Sayyidatnā Maryam*).[12]

---

[10] "Lord Jesus Christ Son of God, have mercy on me a sinner", usually shortened to "Christ have mercy" (*Christe 'eléisòn*).

[11] One of the greatest Catholic practitioners of the invocation of the Holy Name in post-Medieval times was Saint Bernardino of Siena (fifteenth century).

[12] See "The Virginal Doctrine" in *Form and Substance in the*

And make mention, in the Book, of Mary, when she withdrew from her people to a chamber (in the Temple) facing east, and chose seclusion from them. And We sent unto her Our Spirit (Gabriel), and he took before her the form of a perfect man. And she said: "I take refuge from thee in the All-Merciful. If thou art God-fearing." He said: "I am but a messenger of thy Lord, that I may bestow on thee a holy son." She said: "How can I have a son when no mortal hath touched me, neither have I been unchaste?" He said: "So it shall be. Thy Lord hath said: 'Easy is this for Me. And We will make of him a sign for mankind and a mercy from Us. It is a thing decreed.'" And she conceived him, and retired with him to a far-off place. And the throes came upon her by the trunk of the palm-tree. She said: "Would that I had died ere this, and become a thing forgotten!" Then one cried unto her from below her: "Grieve not! Thy Lord hath placed a rivulet beneath thee, and shake the trunk of the palm-tree toward thee, thou wilt cause ripe dates to fall upon thee. So eat and drink and be consoled" (*Sūra* "Mary", 19:16-26).

The second passage is the following:

Whenever Zachariah went into the sanctuary (*mihrāb*) where she was, he found her supplied with food. "O Mary," he said, "whence hast thou this?" She said, "It is from God. Verily God supplieth whom He will without reckoning" (*Sūra* "The Family of 'Imrān", 3:37).

Religions (Bloomington, IN: World Wisdom, 2002), pp. 113-114.

In this interpretation, the "shaking of the palm-tree" symbolizes the "active" virtues, and above all, *dhikr*. "Withdrawal into the *mihrāb*" symbolizes the "passive" virtues, and above all, *faqr*.

The Koranic references to Jesus are also numerous. For the Koran, Jesus is the Messiah, the incarnate Word of God (4:171), the son of Mary ever-Virgin (21:91), who was sent by God to confirm the Pentateuch with the Gospel, which is guidance and light (5:46). Mary and her son have deserved the admiration of the Universe (21:91). "Every son of Adam, at birth is touched by Satan, save only the son of Mary and his Mother" (*hadīth*). The Koran makes specific mention of the resurrection of Christ (4:156-158; 19:33). As mentioned earlier, whereas Mohammed is referred to as the "Seal of Prophecy" (*khātim an-nubuwwa*), Christ is referred to by some Sufis as the "Seal of Sanctity" (*khātim al-wilāya*). In his celebrated work *Al-Futūhāt al-Makkīya* ("The Meccan Revelations", II:64-66), Muhyi 'd-Dīn ibn 'Arabī comments on this as follows:

> The Seal of universal holiness, above which there is no other holy, is our Lord Jesus. We have met several contemplatives of the heart of Jesus. . . . I myself have been united to him several times in my ecstasies, and by his ministry I returned to God at my conversion. . . . He has given me the name of friend and has prescribed austerity and nakedness of spirit.

*

* *

The highest state of mystical union or "the Supreme Identity" has been expressed in many different ways. Sometimes such expressions, when in subjective mode, are arrestingly direct. One thinks of Saint Paul's "Not I, but Christ in me" and Al-Hallāj's "I am the Truth" (*anā 'l-Haqq*). In objective mode, there is the Hindu *Tat tvam asi* ("thou art That") and there is the Buddhist assertion that *samsāra* (the relative) is *Nirvāna* (the Absolute). (but not the other way round! An analogous point was made in the first paragraph on p. 36 in connection with the question of pantheism). The reference here is to the "oneness of being" between the creature and the Creator. *Qui adhaeret Deo, unus spiritus est* ("But he that is joined unto the Lord is one spirit") (1 Cor. 6:17).

One of the expressions of the Supreme Identity found in Hinduism and Buddhism is that of Tantra, which makes use of the symbolism of sexual union (*maithuna*). This symbolism is often the subject of Hindu and Buddhist statuary. In the Hindu form,[13] it is basically a question of the union of Shiva (God) with His Shakti or Consort— representing his own creative "Powers" or "Energies", separated from Him, nonetheless, in so far as He is infinite and "unqualified" (*nirguna*).[14] Shiva and his Shakti are the divine prototypes of *purusha* and *prakriti*, which can be translated into Western scholastic terms as Essence and Substance, or Act and Potency.

The first of these two terms represents the Active Pole, and the second the Passive Pole, of universal manifestation. Each of these Poles has "dynamic" and "static" modes. For example, in Medieval terms, the dynamic mode of the Passive Pole is *Natura* and the static mode of the

---

[13] In the Buddhist form, it is a question of the "marriage of Wisdom (*prajñā*) and Method (*upāya*)".

[14] This is reminiscent of the doctrine of the "Divine Energies" (*dynameis*) of Saint Gregory Palamas.

Passive Pole is *Materia*.[15] In Tantra, it is characteristically a question of the union between the static mode of the Active Pole and the dynamic mode of the Passive Pole. We are here on the threshold of the mystery of Creation itself. It is this creative process that is reflected in all traditional art. In the words of Saint Thomas Aquinas: "Art is the imitation of Nature (*Natura*) in her mode of operation." This is, precisely, the dynamic mode of the Passive Pole.

The Two Poles of Universal Manifestation: "Essence" and "Substance" (*Purusha* and *Prakriti* or *Yang* and *Yin* in their two modes)

This diagram indicates meanings of the pairs passive/active and static/dynamic, as well as the metaphysical basis of the relationship between the sexes.

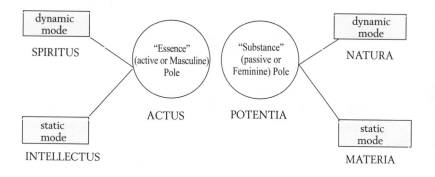

[15] The dynamic and static aspects of the Active Pole are respectively *Spiritus* and *Intellectus*, and the dynamic and passive aspects of the Passive Pole are *Natura* and *Materia*. This exposition is taken from Titus Burckhardt's *Alchemy* (Louisville, KY: Fons Vitae, 1997), chap. 9, "'Nature Can Overcome Nature'."

In mysticism, of the "Tantric" type, it is not merely a question of the union of Active and Passive, or dynamic and static. It is specifically a union of the dynamic mode of the Passive Pole (NATURA) with the static mode of the active pole (INTELLECTUS). At the same time, there is also a union of the dynamic mode of the Active Pole (SPIRITUS) and the static mode of the Passive Pole (MATERIA).

The unique strength of the bond comes precisely from the union of "static" Activity with "dynamic" Passivity. The intimacy of this union is reflected in many arts. It is particularly clear, for example, in the symbolism of weaving, where the warp and the weft stand in a "sexual" relationship to one another. "The weft" (dynamic, but nevertheless—because horizontal—passive and feminine) "darts in and out of the warp" (static, but nevertheless—because vertical—active and masculine) "like a streak of lightning or an arrow speeding to its mark; like a ship, it plies from shore to shore, out and home again; like Lakshmī casting flowers in Vishnu's lap, it adorns and nourishes its Lord."[16]

The expression "static Activity" recalls the Taoist concept of the "actionless Act",[17] and indeed the doctrine of Tantra is well expressed in the Taoist symbol of Yin-Yang. The Active (or masculine) Pole, Yang, is represented by a white field, but his "motionlessness" is represented by a black spot in the center. The Passive (or feminine) Pole, Yin, is represented by a black field, but her "dynamism" is represented by a white spot. The intimacy of their union

[16]   Aristide Messinesi, "A Craft as a Fountain of Grace and a Means of Realization", in *Art and Thought: A Tribute to Ananda Coomaraswamy* (London: Luzac, 1947), p. 38.

[17]   Cf. the "motionless Mover" of Aristotle.

and the strength of their bond are represented by the sinuous intertwining (reminiscent of a Tantric statue) of the two fields, in the well-known symbol:

Incidentally, a black field, taken by itself, and with the white spot in its center, vividly recalls the Black Virgin of Christian iconography. One thinks, for example, of the celebrated black Madonna (with the Child Jesus) at Czenstochowa in Poland. In Christian terms, spiritual realization—or rather, "actualization" (in the terms of Scholastic philosophy)—is the "passage from Potency to Act".

All these considerations have not taken us away from our main theme, namely, the mystical path, and spiritual realization, in Sufism.[18] The Active and Passive Poles, and their union, are central to Sufi doctrine and method. In Sufi writings, the Polarity in question appears as the Divine Command (*al-Amr*) and Universal Nature (*at-Tabī'at al-*

---

[18] The numerous references to non-Islamic mysticisms in this section on Sufism have been introduced, firstly, because all religions are now on our doorstep and it is important to know something about them, and, secondly, because expounding a particular principle in terms of another religion can often throw light on the same principle when it occurs in the religion under study. Mohammed said: "Seek knowledge even if it be in China!"

kulliya); and again as the Supreme Pen (*al-Qalam*) and the Guarded Tablet (*al-Lauh al-mahfūz*).[19] This relationship is at the heart of Islamic metaphysics, while in mysticism (as well as in art), use is made of the fact that the "creating" pathway leading from Principle to manifestation is also the "re-integrating" pathway leading from manifestation to Principle.

The application of the "sexual" symbolism may sometimes be reversed, and there are some Sufis who attribute femininity, not to the Passive Pole of manifestation, but to the Divine Essence (*Dhāt*).[20] This has above all a "mystical" or "operative" end in view, the goal of the mystical quest being personified as a woman, usually named Laila which means "night" (again a reference to the Divine Essence).[21] "This is the holiest and most secret inwardness of God, and marks the end of the mystical path."[22] In this symbolism Laila and *haqīqa* (Divine Reality) are one. The Virgin Mary (*Sayyidatnā Maryam*), who personifies not only all the virtues but also Divine Mercy (*Rahma*), is identified by some Sufis with Laila. It is not surprising that many Sufi poems take the form of love lyrics. The name Laila is also that of the heroine of the best-known love story of the Muslim world, "Laila and Majnūn".

---

[19] See Titus Burckhardt, *Introduction to Sufi Doctrine* (Bloomington, IN: World Wisdom, 2008), chap. 5.

[20] In Arabic, *Dhāt* ("Essence") is feminine in gender.

[21] This "subjective" attitude is not unrelated to the "objective" doctrine of *Sat-Chit-Ānanda* seen as "Beloved-Lover-Love". Likewise, in the Buddhist form of Tantra, it is Wisdom (*prajñā*) which is feminine and Method (*upāya*) which is masculine.

[22] Martin Lings, "Sufism", in *Man, Myth, and Magic*, No. 97, p. 2713 (London, 1972).

It goes without saying, of course, that in the "ordinary" relationship between the human soul and God, the soul is passive and "feminine", while God is active and "masculine". It is in the mystical path that the symbolic relationship may sometimes be reversed.

Typical Islamic geometrical design
(based on the "pentacle") from
the 'Attarīn Medersa, Fez, Morocco

ASPECTS OF ISLAMIC ESOTERISM[1]

Esoterism is the correlative of exoterism. The latter is the outward and general religion of dogmas and observances, to which, in a traditional society, the whole community adheres, and which promises, and provides the means for achieving, salvation. The former is the "total truth" behind—and symbolically expressed by—the dogmas of the general religion and at the same time it is the key to, and the reason for being of, the religious observances. What, in exoterism, are dogmas and commandments, become, in esoterism, truths and ways of realization. In both exoterism and esoterism the same two poles are necessarily present: theory and practice, or doctrine and method; they are simply envisaged at different levels. The first of these two poles, incidentally, clearly has a primary role or function: one must understand. before one can do. Any practice without true theory lacks meaning and efficacy.

Exoterisrn is interested: it aims at transforming the collectivity, and saving as many souls as possible. Esoter-

---

[1] This article was written at a different time from, and elaborates on some of the ideas contained in, the preceding treatise on Sufism. In so doing, some repetitions are inevitable.

65

ism is disinterested and impersonal. As "total truth", it "saves" *a fortiori*,[2] but whereas exoterism, to be itself, inevitably has a moralizing and to some extent a subjectivist character, esoterism is dispassionate and totally objective.

The "universalist" point of view can perhaps best be expressed by the saying: "All religions come from God, and all religions lead back to God". The first clause refers to doctrine, and the second to method (or "way" or "path"). This saying presupposes that it is a question of an orthodox and traditional religion, which has not undergone any fundamental alteration.

The various revealed religions are sometimes represented as sectors of a circle, the sectors, by definition, coming together at the central point. The larger and wider area of the sector, bordering on the circumference, represents a given exoterism; the smaller and narrower area of the sector that is close to the center is the corresponding esoterism; and the dimensionless center itself is esoterism in the pure state: the total truth. The same symbolism can also be represented in three dimensions, in the form of a cone or a mountain. Here it will be said that "all paths lead to the same summit". Once again, the dimensionless central point (this time the summit of the mountain) represents the total truth. The cone or the mountain is made up of sectors, each one of which represents a religion. The lower slopes of each sector represent a given exoterism, while the upper slopes of the same sector represent the corresponding esoterism. The summit represents esoterism in the pure state.

Perhaps the most direct of all the symbolisms referring to the genesis, mutual relationship, and saving role, of the

---

[2] "Ye shall know the truth, and the truth shall make you free" (John 8:32).

various revelations, is that which likens esoterism (in the pure state) to the uncolored light, and the various religions to red, green, yellow, and the other colors of the spectrum. Depending on their distance from the source of light, the colored rays will be more intense or more weak (i.e. more esoteric or more exoteric). Each color is a form or a vehicle of the truth. Each color "represents" the total truth. But the supra-formal total truth, the plenitude of uncolored light, is not exhausted by, or limited to, one single color. Incidentally, this symbolism has the merit of showing, amongst other things, just how precious exoterism is. A weak colored light shining in unfavorable circumstances is in itself sufficient (if we genuinely try to see by it) to save us from surrounding darkness. Despite "refraction" (and let us remember that it is precisely its "color" which makes it accessible to the majority of men), and despite its weakness, it is the same light as the uncolored light of God, and its merciful role is precisely to lead us back to its own absolute and infinite source.

Terminologically one may regard "esoterism" and "mysticism" as synonymous. The term "spirituality", may also be used in the same sense. Mysticism is known to be the inward or spiritual dimension within every religion, and this is precisely what esoterism is. This may prompt the question: does the mystic who has reached the end of the path (who has achieved "salvation", "liberation", or "enlightenment") leave religion behind? To this the answer must be yes and no. Returning to our symbolism of the uncolored light which is refracted into many colors, one may say that he has left "color" behind, but not light. And yet, when one recalls that each color is fully present in the uncolored light (in harmonious union with all the other colors in what amounts to a principial plenitude of light), one cannot truly say that he has left color behind either. What he has done is to trace his own color back to its essence or source, where, although infinitely clarified, it is essentially and abundantly present. The uncolored light, source of all the colors, has also been called the *philosophia perennis* (perennial philosophy) or *religio perennis* (perennial religion). This is one with what was called above esoterism in the pure state.

And this has an important practical consequence for the spiritual traveler. One cannot take the view that, since mysticism or esoterism is the inner truth common to all the religions, one can dispense with religion (exoterism) and seek only mysticism (esoterism). Man's situation is such that with God's grace, he may be made worthy of turning towards the uncolored light only if he approaches it by way of "red" or "green" or some other color. To believe that we can reach the uncolored light without proceeding along a "colored ray" is in practice an illusion.

One should perhaps also say at this point that facile and superficial syncretism (such as that of the Theosophical Society or the "New Age" movement, with their hotchpotch of beliefs) is also a vain enterprise. To pick and choose bits and pieces from each religion (allegedly those relating to an imagined "highest common factor") is to try to mix the immiscible. It leads not to clarity, but to opacity.

*
* *

In the foregoing symbolisms, the relationships between Islamic exoterism, Islamic esoterism, and the *religio perennis* become apparent. Islamic exoterism, which corresponds to the *shari'a* (the outward law), is the corpus of religious beliefs and practices that shapes the community and leads individuals in it towards salvation. On the other hand, Islamic esoterism or Sufism (in Arabic *tasawwuf*), is the inward or spiritual dimension of the religion, and is the concern only of those possessed of the appropriate vocation. The Koran declares: "Verily we are God's and unto Him do we return" (*Sūra* "The Cow", 2:156). This verse of course applies to all—both to Sufism and the general religion. The difference between them is as follows: esoterism is based either on understanding ("Knowledge" or *ma'rifa*) or on "Love" (*mahabba*), whereas exoterism is based on will, merit, or "Fear" (that is, Fear of God, *makhāfa*). In the "Way of Fear", the gulf between "slave" and "Lord" is never abandoned. In the "Way of Love", the soul moves beyond "slavehood" (*'ubūdiya*) and becomes becomes a "friend" (*walī*). In the "Way of Knowledge", the goal is union with the Divine Essence, whatever be the degree or mode of this union.

Let it be added that all religions teach that "perdition" or "damnation" is the result, precisely, of the individual's refusing his co-operation with the divine will as expressed, for example, in the respective religious revelation. Revelation represents the "objective" pole of religion, in that it comes to the individual from outside. The "subjective" pole is that which comes to the individual from within. It includes both the voice of conscience and also that intuitive assent to the truths of religion which constitutes faith. For religion and spirituality, revelation and faith are the twin sources, objective and subjective respectively, of "Fear", "Love", and "Knowledge" of God.

One of the most easily graspable keys to the origin and meaning of the concepts "objective" and "subjective" is furnished by the Hindu doctrine of *Sat-Chit-Ānanda*. In Hinduism, this term is one of the names of God. Its constituent elements are usually translated as Being, Consciousness, and Bliss. This enables us to see that Being is the Divine Object, Consciousness the Divine Subject, while Bliss—the joyous coming together of the two—is Divine Union. The most "essential" translation, therefore, of *Sat-Chit-Ānanda* is "Object-Subject-Union". This is the model and origin of all possible objects and subjects, and of the longing of the latter for the former.[3]

This trinitarian aspect of the Divinity is universal and is to be found in all religions. In Christianity it is the central dogma: God viewed as Father, Son, and Holy Spirit. The analogy between the Christian Trinity and "Being-Consciousness-Bliss" is best seen in the doctrinal expositions of the Greek Fathers and also in Saint Augustine's designation of the Christian Trinity as "Being-Wisdom-Life", which carries the same connotation of "Object-Subject-Union".

In Islam, although it is the religion of strict monotheism, certain Sufi formulations evoke the trinitarian aspect of the Divinity. Reference has been made in the previous chapter to the question of "spiritual realization" in Sufism, the essential means of which is the practice of the invocation (*dhikr*) of the Revealed Name of God. In this connection it is said that God is not only That which is invoked (*Madhkūr*), but also, in the last analysis, That within us which invokes (*Dhākir*), and furthermore, that *Dhikr* itself, being one with the internal Activity of God,[4] is also Divine. We thus have the ternary *Madhkūr-Dhākir-Dhikr*, meaning "Invoked-Invoker-Invocation", the relationship of these elements to one another being precisely that of "Object-Subject-Union". This is the very essence of the theory and practice of esoterism—Islamic or other—for this "Union" *in divinis* is the prefiguration of, and the pattern for, the union of man with the Divine. Hindu,

---

[3] *Sat-Chit-Ānanda* may also be interpreted as "Known-Knower-Knowledge" or "Beloved-Lover-Love".

[4] That this Divine Act should pass through man is the mystery of salvation.

Christian, and Sufi doctrines coincide in elucidating just why this is so.

*

* *

The mystery of union, from whichever doctrinal point of view it may be approached, carries an inescapable "operative" implication and is the basis of the mystical path and the motivation for all spiritual striving. One of the most esoteric of all doctrines expressing the mystery of union is that concerning the Logos. This doctrine has its origin in the distinction, within God Himself, between God and the Godhead, or between "Being" and "Beyond-Being" (or "Divine Essence"). This distinction is to be found in the esoterisms of several religions, and is made explicit in the treatises of such great "gnostics" as Shankara (in Hinduism), Eckhart (in Christianity), and Ibn 'Arabī (in Islam). Ordinary theology distinguishes simply between God and man, between the Uncreated and the created. But in each of these categories, esoterism makes a distinction. For example, within God Himself, there is already a prefiguration of creation, and this is God as "Being". God as "Being" is the immediate Creator of the world. This is the source of the metaphysical distinction between "Beyond-Being" ("Essence") and "Being", or between the Godhead and the Personal God. Likewise, within the created, there is a distinction to be made. There is something within the created itself, which reflects the Uncreated (something, within the relative, which reflects the Absolute). For Christianity, this is the Savior; for Islam, the Koran. In more general terms, it is truth and virtue, or symbol and sacrament. (See the table and the diagram on the "Five Divine Presences" on pp. 31-32.)

These different strands are brought together in the concept of the Logos: the prefiguration of the created in the Uncreated (the Personal God) is the *uncreated* Logos. The reflection of the Uncreated in the created, or of the Absolute in the relative—namely: Savior; Prophet; truth and virtue; symbol and sacrament—is the *created* Logos. Hence the indispensability of the Logos (with its two faces) as the "bridge" between created and Uncreated, or between man and God.

Without the Logos, no contact between man and God would be possible. This seems to be the position of the Deists. Without the Logos, there would be a fundamental dualism, not Non-Dualism" (*Advaita*), as the Vedantists call it. This indeed is the blind alley that Descartes (with his unbridgeable dichotomy of "spirit and matter") has led us into.

Esoterism thus renders explicit the reality of mystical union, for it is by uniting himself with the "created" Logos (for example, in the Christian Eucharist, or in the Islamic Invocation of the Divine Name, coupled with the practice of the essential virtues), that the spiritual aspirant (the *faqīr*, as he is called in Islam) realizes his union with, or reintegration into, the uncreated Divinity. For a full exposition of the role of the virtues in spiritual realization, see pp. 56-58.

The Logos is one, it is everywhere and always the same, but it has many different personifications or manifestations. Each of these is "unique" within its own religion, often in the shape of the Founder. Jesus and Mohammed are personifications of the Logos, and this is what enables them to speak in such absolute terms. Mohammed said: "He that has seen me has seen God". That is, whoever has seen the created (and visible) Logos has, sacramentally, also "seen" the uncreated (and invisible) Logos, namely God as "Being" or Creator (in contradistinction from God as Beyond-Being, the Eckhartian "Godhead"). Similarly, Jesus said: "No man cometh to the Father but by me"

(John 14:6). This has the same meaning. It is for this precise reason that Mohammed for Muslims (like Jesus for Christians) is "absolutely" indispensable. In Islam, this is the ultimate, or esoteric, reason for conformity to the *Sunna*, the "Wont" or "Practice" of the Prophet. Outwardly the *Sunna* constitutes a norm for the whole Islamic community, but for the *faqīr*, conformity to the "inward" or essential *Sunna* is as it were a "sacrament", and a central mode of realizing union.

Mutatis mutandis the Virgin Mary plays the same role. She is the feminine personification of the Logos—or the personification of the feminine aspects of the Logos, namely Purity, Beauty, and Goodness. This is why, in Catholicism, she is called "Co-Redemptrix".

The above doctrinal considerations let it be seen that mystical union, whatever be its degree or mode, is realizable only through the Logos.[5]

*

* *

It has been mentioned more than once that Sufism is the spiritual and metaphysical interpretation of the religion of Islam. The central doctrine of Islam is the "testimony of faith" (*Shahāda*): "There is no god but God; Mohammed is the Messenger of God" (*la ilāha illā 'Llāh; Muhammadun Rasūlu 'Llāh*). The esoteric interpretation of the *Shahāda* generally takes the form of the doctrine known as *wahdat al-wujūd*, or the "oneness of being". According to this, the *Shahāda* means not merely that "there is no god but God"; it can also be expressed as "there is no reality except Reality". One of the names of God, indeed, is *al-*

---

[5] This exposition is taken from the writings of Frithjof Schuon. See especially, *Esoterism as Principle and as Way*.

Haqq, which means "Reality" or "Truth".

This doctrine also means that the relative has no reality other than in the Absolute, and the finite has no reality other than in the Infinite. The Muslim or the Sufi has access to the Absolute and the Infinite in the Koran (God's revealed word), in the *Shahāda*, and, most intensely of all, in the Divine Name, *Allāh*. He also has access through the Prophet who, within the world itself, is God's very reflection. The Prophet's name is communicated in the second clause of the *Shahāda*. Thus through these two revealed and sacred clauses, man has access, on the one hand, to the Divine Immutability and, on the other, to the Mohammedian or Prophetic Norm. In and through the two *Shahādas*, the imperfect is overwhelmed by the Perfect (the Mohammedian Norm), and the impermanent is extinguished by the Permanent (God Himself). As the Koran says: "Truth hath come, and falsehood hath vanished. Verily falsehood is ever bound to vanish" (*Sūra* "The Night Journey", 17:81).[6]

*
* *

The above considerations enable us to see how the spiritual method, or means of realization, in Sufism is above all the "remembrance of God" (*dhikr Allāh*). The verbal root concerned also means "to mention" or "to invoke", and the practice is sometimes called "invocation" (i.e. the invocation of the Divine Name). Reference was made to this above. This spiritual practice is derived from numerous Koranic injunctions, amongst which are:

---

[6] For a detailed esoteric interpretation of the *Shahāda*, see "Concerning the '*Barzakh*'" in *The Essential Titus Burckhardt* (Bloomington, IN: World Wisdom, 2003).

Remember God with much remembrance (*idhkurū 'Llāha dhikran kathīran*) (*Sūra* "The Confederates", 33:41).

Verily in the remembrance of God do hearts find rest (*a lā bi-dhikri 'Llāhi tatma'innu 'l-qulūb*) (*Sūra* "The Thunder", 13:28).

Remember Me and I will remember you (*idhkurū-nī, adhkur-kum*) (*Sūra* "The Cow", 2:152).

Dhikr may be performed only with the permission and guidance of a spiritual master or Sheikh. It can be performed either in solitude or in a gathering (*majlis*) of *fuqarā* (plural of *faqīr*) convened for that purpose, and led by a Sheikh or his representative (*muqaddam*). From another point of view, *dhikr* should, in principle, be constant. This is analogous to the "prayer without ceasing" (1 Thess. 5:17) of Saint Paul (the Jesus-Prayer of the Eastern Church) and to the *japa-yoga* of the Hindus.

As explained in the previous chapter, *dhikr*, in the wider sense, includes any devotion that serves as a support for the remembrance of God, in particular the *wird*, or rosary, which most *fuqarā* recite morning and evening, using a *tasbih* or chaplet. The *wird* comprises three Koranic formulas, each of which is recited one hundred times. The first formula, asking for forgiveness, pertains to the individual and its aim is to establish contrition and resolution. The second formula contains the name of the Prophet, and seeks to confer on the *faqīr* the perfection pertaining to the human state as it was created. The third formula contains the Name of God, and enshrines and vehicles the mystery of Union. The three formulas thus correspond to the three "stages" known in the mysticisms of various religions, namely: purification, perfection, union. In their essence, these correspond to the three fundamental aspects of all spirituality: humility, charity, veracity.

These last three words lead us once more to the ternary, *makhāfa, mahabba,* and *ma'rifa*: the "Fear of God", "Love of God", and "Knowledge of God". These spiritual attitudes may be regarded either as simultaneous aspects or successive stages. They correspond to the Hindu ternary: *karma- mārga* (the Way of Action), *bhakti-mārga* (the Way of Love), and *jñāna-mārga* (the Way of Knowledge, or "gnosis"[7]). Strictly speaking, it is only *bhakti* and *jñāna* (i.e. *mahabba* and *ma'rifa*) that constitute esoterism: esoterism is either a Way of Love, or a Way of Knowledge, or a combination of both.

Since comparisons with Christianity may be useful, let us recall the incident in the life of Christ when he was received in the house of the sisters Martha and Mary (Luke 10:38-42). What has come to be known in Christianity as the "Way of Martha" corresponds to *karma-mārga*, the way of religious observance and good works. The esoteric or mystical way, on the other hand, is the "Way of Mary", which comprises two modes, namely *bhakti-mārga* (the Way of Love) and *jñāna-marga* (the Way of Knowledge). *Karma* as such is purely exoteric, but it is important to stress that there is always a karmic component within both *bhakti* and *jñāna*. Sufism teaches quite explicitly that the Way of Love (*mahabba*) and the Way of Knowledge (*ma'rifa*) both necessarily contain an element of Fear or conformity (*makhāfa*). Likewise the Way of Knowledge invariably contains within it the reality of Love. As for the Way of Love, which is composed of faith and devotion,

---

[7] This word is used purely etymologically, and is not a reference to the current, in the early history of Christianity, known as "gnosticism". "Gnosis", from the Greek, is the only adequate English rendering for the Sanskrit *jñāna* (with which in fact it is cognate) and the Arabic *ma'rifa*.

it contains an indirect element of *jñāna* or *ma'rifa* in the form of dogmatic and speculative theology. This element is in the intellectual speculation as such, and not in its object which, for the Way of Love, is restricted to God as "Being", "Creator", or "Lord". When the object is God as "Beyond-Being" or "Essence", it is no longer a case of *bhakti* (or *mahabba*), but of *jñāna* (or *ma'rifa*).

In both the Way of Love and the Way of Knowledge, the element "Beauty" is of the greatest importance. It is plays a role in all spiritualities, including Sufism. It is particularly important for the *jñānin* (or *'arif bi'Llāh*), in whom it evokes an aspiration towards contemplative Peace and unifying Love.

In spite of the presence in each "Way" of elements of the two others, the three Ways *karma*, *bhakti*, and *jñāna* (or *makhāfa*, *mahabba*, and *ma'rifa*) represent three specific and easily distinguishable modes of religious aspiration.

As for the question as to which of these paths a given aspirant adheres to, it is overwhelmingly a matter of temperament and vocation. It is a case where the Way chooses the individual and not the individual the Way.

Historically speaking, Christian mysticism has been characterized in the main by the "Way of Love", whereas Islamic mysticism (like Hindu mysticism) comprises both the "Way of Love" and the "Way of Knowledge". The language of the "Way of Love" has a remarkably similar ring in whichever mysticism it crops up, but the more "gnostic" formulations of Islamic esoterism (as of Vedanta), strike a foreign note in the ears of those who are familiar only with Christian, or at any rate bhaktic, forms of spirituality.[8]

---

[8] Those who, by way of exception, have manifested the "Way of Knowledge" in Christianity include such great figures as Dionysius the Areopagite, Meister Eckhart, and Angelus Silesius. It

The fact that the spiritual method *par excellence* consists in "sacramental" concentration on the revealed Name of God (*dhikr Allāh*) indicates clearly that the practical side of Islamic esoterism is the very opposite of giving free play to man's unregenerate subjectivity. Indeed, it amounts to the exposing of his unregenerate subjectivity to the normative and transforming influence of the Divine "Object", God transcendent. At the same time, and even more esoterically, it is the exposing of man's paltry egoism, seen in turn as an "object" (illusorily other than God), to the withering and yet quickening influence of the Divine "Subject", God immanent; the Name of God (*Allāh*) being both transcendent Object and immanent Subject (*Madhkūr* and *Dhākir*). These two contrasting attitudes or "stations" (*maqām, maqāmāt*)— spiritual extinction before the Divine Object and spiritual rebirth in the Divine Subject—are the two aspects, objective and subjective, of unitive Knowledge (*ma'rifa*).[9] In Sufi treatises, they have been called, respectively, *fanā* (extinction) and *baqā* (permanence).

is significant that it is precisely the works of "gnostics" such as these that have tended to cause ripples in the generally "bhaktic" climate of Christianity.

[9]   This synthesis of the dual aspects of spiritual realization is taken from the writings of Frithjof Schuon. See especially *The Eye of the Heart*, chapter "Microcosm and Symbol" (Bloomington, IN: World Wisdom, 1997).

APPENDIX

QUOTATIONS RELATING TO SUFISM

The Koran

In the Name of God, the Clement, the Merciful,
Praise be to God, the Lord of the worlds, The Clement,
  the Merciful,
The owner of the Day of Judgement,
Thee we worship and in Thee we seek refuge.
Guide us upon the straight path
The path of those to whom Thou art gracious,
Not of those upon whom Thine anger hath fallen,
Nor of those who are astray.
Amen.

Sūra "The Opening", 1:1-7

He (God) is the First and the Last, the Outward and the
Inward.

Sūra "Iron", 57:3

Wheresoever ye may turn, there is the Face of God.

Sūra "The Cow", 2:115

We (God) are nearer to him (man) than his jugular vein.

Sūra "Qaf", 50:16

God is the light of the Heavens and the earth.
Sūra "Light", 24:35

All on the earth shall pass away; there abideth but the Face of thy Lord, resplendent with Majesty and Bounty.
Sūra "The All-Merciful", 55:26-27

Men whom neither trade nor profit diverts from the remembrance of God.
Sūra "Light", 24:37

Say: *Allāh*, and leave them to their idle prattle.
Sūra "Cattle", 6:91

And bear with those who call on their Lord, morning and evening, seeking His Face.
Sūra "The Cave", 18:28

And in the earth are portents for those whose faith is sure, and also in your souls. Can ye then not see?
Sūra "The Winnowing Winds", 51:20-21

We shall show them Our signs on the horizons and in their souls, until it is clear to them that it is the Truth. Doth it not suffice as to thy Lord, that He is witness over all things?
Sūra "The Expounded", 41:53

Verily we created the Heavens and the earth with naught but Truth, yet most men know not.
Sūra "Smoke", 44:38-39

If my slaves ask thee of Me, say I am near. I answer the prayer of the pray-er when he prayeth.
Sūra "The Cow", 2:186

God guides to His Light whomsoever He pleases.
Sūra "Light", 24:35

Verily God giveth beyond measure to whom He will.
Sūra "The Family of 'Imrān", 3:37

And say: Truth has come and falsehood has vanished. Verily falsehood is ever bound to vanish.
Sūra "The Children of Israel", 17:81

And We have revealed the Koran, which is a healing and a mercy for believers.
Sūra "The Children of Israel", 17:82

And seek aid, through patience and prayer.
Sūra "The Cow", 2:45

Fear God, for it is God Who teaches you.
Sūra "The Cow", 2:282

They seek to extinguish God's light with their mouths, but though the unbelievers hate it, God will perfect His light. He it is who sent His Messenger with guidance and the religion of the Truth.
Sūra "The Ranks", 61:8-9

There is no refuge from God but in Him.
Sūra "Repentance", 9:118

Keep vigil all the night, save a little.
Sūra "The Enshrouded One", 73:2

Glorify Him the whole night through.
Sūra "Man", 76:26

Flee unto God.

Sūra "The Winnowing Winds", 51:50

The seven heavens and the earth and all that is therein praise Him, and there is not a thing but hymneth His praise; but ye understand not their praise. Verily He is ever kind, forgiving.

Sūra "The Children of Israel", 17:44

O men! Ye are the poor (*fuqarā*) in relation to God, and God is the Rich (*Ghanī*) to whom all praises are due.

Sūra "The Creator", 35:15

It is not their eyes that are blind, but their hearts.

Sūra "The Pilgrimage", 22:46

Verily we are God's and unto Him we shall return.

Sūra "The Cow", 2:156

Mohammed

I was a hidden treasure, and I wished to be known, so I created the world.

hadīth qudsī[1]

Verily My mercy precedeth My wrath.

hadīth qudsī

Nothing is more pleasant to Me, as a means for My slave to draw nigh unto Me, than the worship that I have made

---

[1] As mentioned previously, a *hadīth* (plural *ahādīth*) is a saying of Mohammed. A *hadīth qudsī* ("sacred saying") is a direct saying of God (in which He speaks in the first person) revealed to Mohammed, but not constituting a part of the Koran.

binding upon him; and My slave ceaseth not to draw near unto Me by devotions of his free will until I love him; and when I love him, I am the hearing whereby he heareth and the sight whereby he seeth and the hand wherewith he smiteth and the foot whereon he walketh.

hadīth qudsī

My Heaven cannot contain Me, nor can My earth, but the heart of My believing slave can contain Me.

hadīth qudsī

God saith: Whoso doeth one good act, for him are ten rewards: and I also give more to whomever I will; and whoso doeth an ill, its punishment is equal to it, or I forgive him; and whoso seeketh to approach Me one span, I approach him one cubit; and whoso seeketh to approach Me one cubit, I approach him two fathoms; and whoso walketh towards Me, I run towards him; and whoso cometh before Me with an earth full of sins, and believeth solely in Me, him I come before with a face of forgiveness as big as the earth.

hadīth qudsī

Worship God as if thou sawest Him, for if thou seest Him not, verily He seeth thee.

All that is beautiful comes from the beauty of God.

Everything on earth is accursed, except the remembrance of God.

The heart of man is the Throne of God.

There is no strength and no power but in God.

No one shall meet *Allāh* who has not first met the Prophet.

He who has seen me (the Prophet), has seen the Truth (God).

Made worthy of love to me are perfumes and women, and there has been made a coolness for my eyes in prayer.

Our Lord—may He be blessed and exalted—comes down every night towards the earthly heavens at the time when there remains but the last third of the night, and He says:

"Who calls upon Me, that I may reply to Him? Who asks of Me something, that I may grant his request? Who asks of Me forgiveness, that I may forgive him?"

Whoso knoweth himself, knoweth his Lord.

Be in this world as a stranger or as a passer-by.

God hath ninety-nine Names; he that reciteth them shall enter Paradise.

Whenever men gather together to invoke *Allāh*, they are surrounded by Angels, the Divine Favor envelops them, and Peace (*Sakīna*) descends upon them, and *Allāh* remembers them in His assembly.

For everything there is a polish; and the polish for the heart is the invocation of *Allāh*.

There is no act which takes the punishment of *Allāh* further from you than this invocation.

Whoso protecteth God in his heart, him will God protect in the world.

The *sharī‘a* is what I say (*aqwālī*), the *tarīqa* is what I do (*ā‘amālī*) and the *haqīqa* is what I am (*ahwālī*).

Verily God is beautiful, and He loves beauty

(*Inna 'Llāha jamīlun, yuhibbu'l-jamāl*)
(example of *Thulūth* style of Arabic calligraphy)

The Sufis

Thine existence is a sin wherewith no other sin may be compared.

Rābi‘a al-‘Adawīya (d. 801)

My Lord, eyes are at rest, the stars are setting, hushed are the movements of the birds in their nests, of the monsters in the deep. And Thou art the Just who knoweth no change, the Equity that swerveth not, the Everlasting that passeth not away. The doors of kings are locked and guarded by their henchmen. But Thy door is open to whoso calleth on Thee. My Lord, each lover is now alone with his beloved. And I am alone with Thee.

Rābi‘a al-‘Adawīya

I and Thou signify duality, and duality is an illusion, for Unity alone is Truth (*al-Haqq*, God). When the ego is gone, then God is His own mirror in me.

Abū Yazīd al-Bistāmī (d. 875)

The knowledge of God cannot be obtained by seeking,

but only those who seek it find it.

Abū Yazīd al-Bistāmī

The end of knowledge is that man comes to the point where he was at the origin.

Abū Yazīd al-Bistāmī

I saw my Lord with the eye of the heart. I said: Who art Thou? He answered: Thou.

Mansūr al-Hallāj (d. 922)

O God, drown me in the essence of the Ocean of Divine Solitude, so that I neither see nor hear nor be conscious nor feel except through It.

'Abd as-Salām ibn Mashīsh (d. 1228)

No deed arising from a renouncing heart is small, and no deed arising from an avaricious heart is fruitful.

Ibn 'Atā'illāh (d. 1309)

Everything outside of God is unreal, everything taken individually or collectively, when you truly know it.

Know: without Him the whole creation, including you, would disappear, and come to nothing. Whatever does not have its root in His Being, can in no wise be real.

The knowers of God are as if extinguished. What else can they look upon, but Him, the Transcendent, the Glorious?

Everything they see outside of Him, has truly been destined for destruction, in the past, in the future, and in the present moment. . . .

Abu Madyan (d. 1197)

The Sufi sees his own existence as particles of dust made visible by a ray of sunlight: neither real nor unreal.

Abu'l-Hasan ash-Shādhilī (d. 1258)

Seekest thou Laila [Divine Reality], when she is manifest within thee? Thou deemest her to be other, but she is not other than thou.

Mohammed al-Harrāq (d. 1845)

The beauty of man is in his intelligence and the intelligence of woman is in her beauty.

Sufi saying

Truth melteth like snow in the hands of him whose soul melteth not like snow in the hands of Truth.

attributed to *Ahmad al-'Alawī*

THE NINETY-NINE NAMES OF GOD

"To God belong the most beautiful Names;
invoke Him by them"
(*Wa li 'Llāhi 'l-Asmā'u 'l-husnā, fa 'd'ū-hu bi-hā*)
(*Sūra* "The Heights", 7:180).

Allāh	= God	22. *Al-Khāfiz*	= The Abaser
1. *Ar-Rahmān*	= The Clement	23. *Ar-Rāfi'*	= The Exalter
2. *Ar-Rahīm*	= The Merciful	24. *Al-Mu'izz*	= The Honorer
3. *Al-Malik*	= The King	25. *Al-Muzīl*	= The Abaser
4. *Al-Quddūs*	= The Holy	26. *As-Sāmi'*	= The Hearer
5. *As-Salām*	= The Peace	27. *Al-Basīr*	= The Seer
6. *Al-Mu'min*	= The Faithful	28. *Al-Hākam*	= The Judge
7. *Al-Muhaimin*	= The Protector	29. *Al-'Ādl*	= The Just
8. *Al-'Azīz*	= The Mighty	30. *Al-Latīf*	= The Subtle
9. *Al-Jabbār*	= The Compeller	31. *Al-Khabir*	= The Aware
10. *Al-Mutakabbir*	= The Great	32. *Al-Halīm*	= The Sweet
11. *Al-Khāliq*	= The Creator	33. *Al-'Azīm*	= The Mighty
12. *Al-Bāri'*	= The Maker	34. *Al-Ghafūr*	= The Forgiving
13. *Al-Musawwir*	= The Fashioner	35. *Ash-Shakūr*	= The Grateful
14. *Al-Ghaffār*	= The Forgiver	36. *Al-'Alī*	= The Most High
15. *Al-Qahhār*	= The Dominant	37. *Al-Kabīr*	= The Great
16. *Al-Wahhāb*	= The Bestower	38. *Al-Hāfiz*	= The Preserver
17. *Ar-Razzāq*	= The Provider	39. *Al-Muqīt*	= The Sustainer
18. *Al-Fattāh*	= The Opener	40. *Al-Hasīb*	= The Reckoner
19. *Al-'Alīm*	= The Knower	41. *Al-Jalīl*	= The Majestic
20. *Al-Qābi*	= The Restrainer	42. *Al-Karīm*	= The Generous
21. *Al-Bāsit*	= The Expander	43. *Ar-Raqīb*	= The Watchful

44. *Al-Mujīb*	= The Answerer of Prayers	72. *Al-Awwal*	= The First
45. *Al-Wāsi'*	= The All-Encompassing	73. *Al-Ākhir*	= The Last
46. *Al-Hakīm*	= The Wise	74. *Az-Zāhir*	= The Outward
47. *Al-Wadūd*	= The Loving	75. *Al-Bātin*	= The Inward
48. *Al-Majīd*	= The Glorious	76. *Al-Wālī*	= The Governor
49. *Al-Bā'ith*	= The Resurrector	77. *Al-Muta'ālī*	= The Exalted
50. *Ash-Shahīd*	= The Witness	78. *Al-Barr*	= The Benign
51. *Al-Haqq*	= The Truth	79. *At-Tawwāb*	= The Relenter
52. *Al-Wakīl*	= The Worthy of Trust	80. *Al-Muntaqim*	= The Avenger

44. *Al-Mujīb* = The Answerer of Prayers
45. *Al-Wāsi'* = The All-Encompassing
46. *Al-Hakīm* = The Wise
47. *Al-Wadūd* = The Loving
48. *Al-Majīd* = The Glorious
49. *Al-Bā'ith* = The Resurrector
50. *Ash-Shahīd* = The Witness
51. *Al-Haqq* = The Truth
52. *Al-Wakīl* = The Worthy of Trust
53. *Al-Qawī'* = The Strong
54. *Al-Matīn* = The Firm
55. *Al-Walī* = The Patron
56. *Al-Hamīd* = The Worthy of Praise
57. *Al-Muhsī* = The Appraiser
58. *Al-Mubdī* = The Originator
59. *Al-Mu'īd* = The Restorer
60. *Al-Muhyī* = The Giver of Life
61. *Al-Mumīt* = The Giver of Death
62. *Al-Hayy* = The Living
63. *Al-Qayyūm* = The Self-Subsisting
64. *Al-Wājid* = The Finder
65. *Al-Mājid* = The Noble
66. *Al-Ahad* = The One
67. *As-Samad* = The Eternal
68. *Al-Qādir* = The Powerful
69. *Al-Muqtadir* = The Determiner
70. *Al-Muqaddim* = The Promoted
71. *Al-Mu'akhir* = The Delayer

72. *Al-Awwal* = The First
73. *Al-Ākhir* = The Last
74. *Az-Zāhir* = The Outward
75. *Al-Bātin* = The Inward
76. *Al-Wālī* = The Governor
77. *Al-Muta'ālī* = The Exalted
78. *Al-Barr* = The Benign
79. *At-Tawwāb* = The Relenter
80. *Al-Muntaqim* = The Avenger
81. *Al-'Afū* = The Pardoner
82. *Ar-Ra'ūf* = The Kind
83. *Māliku'l-Mulk* = The King of the Kingdom
84. *Dhu'l-Jalāli wa'l-Ikrām* = Full of Majesty and Bounty
85. *Al-Muqsit* = The Equitable
86. *Al-Jāmi'* = The Gatherer Together
87. *Al-Ghanī* = The Rich
88. *Al-Mughnī* = The Enricher
89. *Al-Mu'ti* = The Giver
90. *Al-Māni'* = The Withholder
91. *Ad-Darr* = The Distresser
92. *An-Nāfi'* = The Profiter
93. *An-Nūr* = The Light
94. *Al-Hādī* = The Guide
95. *Al-Badī'* = The Incomparable
96. *Al-Bāqī* = The Enduring
97. *Al-Warith* = The Inheritor
98. *Ar-Rashīd* = The Right in Guidance
99. *As-Sabūr* = The Patient

SELECT BIBLIOGRAPHY

A. Books on Sufism

Schuon, Frithjof

Understanding Islam. Bloomington, IN: World Wisdom, 2011.
> The best of all explanations of Islam and Sufism.

Sufism: Veil and Quintessence. Bloomington, IN: World Wisdom, 2007.
> A comparison of "historical" and "quintessential" Sufism, with a chapter on the Arab philosophers.

Christianity/Islam: Perspectives on Esoteric Ecumenism. Bloomington, IN: World Wisdom, 2008.
> Contains a penetrating evaluation of the Shī'a schism.

Form and Substance in the Religions. Bloomington, IN: World Wisdom, 2002.
> Includes chapters on Arab rhetoric, and on Sufi attitudes towards Christand the Virgin Mary.

Burckhardt, Titus

Introduction to Sufi Doctrine. Bloomington, IN: World Wisdom, 2008.

An authoritative exposition of the metaphysics of Islam and Sufism.

Fez: City of Islam. Cambridge, UK: Islamic Texts Society, 1992.

In describing the ancient city of Fez, this beautifully illustrated book serves as a general introduction to Islamic civilization, piety, philosophy, and art.

Moorish Culture in Spain. Louisville, KY: Fons Vitae, 1999.

A fascinating book of Muslim Sufis and Christian mystics, of pious Sultans and holy Kings. An open window onto the Middle Ages in Spain. Contains an illuminating chapter on the Arab philosophers.

Lings, Martin

A Sufi Saint of the Twentieth Century. Cambridge, UK: Islamic Texts Society, 1993.

A monograph on the life and teachings of the Algerian Sheikh Ahmad al-'Alawī; contains detailed descriptions of the doctrines and practices of a North African *tarīqa.*

What is Sufism? Cambridge, UK: Islamic Texts Society, 1999.

An excellent survey of the doctrines, spiritual methods, and the great figures in the history of Sufism.

Macnab, Angus

Spain Under the Crescent Moon. Louisville, KY: Fons Vitae, 1999.

A unique book. A stirring account of cultural and religious co-existence in Moorish Spain; includes several chapters on Medieval Spanish Sufism.

Nicholson, R. A.

The Mystics of Islam. Bloomington, IN: World Wisdom, 2002.
> A pioneering work, first published in 1914. An excellent short survey, but, understandably, in the case of an early study, lacking in doctrinal and terminological precision.

Arberry, A.J.

Sufism. London: Allen & Unwin, 1972.
> An excellent historical sketch, but uncritical of some dubious modern movements.

Schimmel, Annemarie

Mystical Dimensions of Islam. Chapil Hill, NC: University of North Carolina Press, 1975.
> An excellent and very comprehensive survey, but too uncritical of certain modern figures.

Stoddart, William

What Do the Religions Say about Each Other? Christian Attitudes towards Islam, Islamic Attitudes towards Christianity. San Rafael, CA: Sophia Perennis, 2008.
> Visions of compatibility and co-existence.

What Does Islam Mean in Today's World? Religion, Politics, Spirituality. Bloomington, IN: World Wisdom, 2012.
> Some modern repercussions.

B. Some Translations of Original Sufi Writings

'Attar, Farīd ad-Dīn (d.c. 1229).

Muslim Saints and Mystics. London: Routledge, 1966.

Extracts from the *Tadhkirat al-Auliyā* ("The Memorial of the Saints").
Translated by A.J. Arberry.

Ibn 'Arabī, Muhyi'd-Dīn (1165-1240).

Sufis of Andalusia. London: Allen & Unwin, 1971.
The *Rūh al-Quds* ("The Spirit of Holiness") and extracts from the *Ad-Durrat al-Fākhira* ("The Precious Pearl").
Translated by R.W.J. Austin.

Ibn 'Atā' illāh (d. 1309).

Sufi Aphorisms. Leiden: Brill, 1973.
The *Kitāb al-Hikam* ("Book of Wisdom").
Translated by Victor Danner.

Rūmī, Jalāl ad-Dīn (1207-1273).

Discourses of Rumi. Richmond: Curzon Press, 1993.
Translated by A.J. Arberry.

Mulay al-'Arabī ad-Darqāwī (c. 1743-1823).

Letters of a Sufi Master. Louisville, KY: Fons Vitae, 1998.
Translated by Titus Burckhardt.
Helpful answers to frequently recurring spiritual problems.

C. Islamic Art

Since Islamic art—at once particular and universal—is like an outward crystallization of Sufism, we list the following beautifully illustrated books:

Burckhardt, Titus

Art of Islam: Language and Meaning. Bloomington, IN:

World Wisdom, 2009.

    In this fine volume, the intellectual principles and the spiritual role of artistic creativity in its various Islamic forms are richly and lucidly presented, accompanied by many beautiful illustrations in color.

Lings, Martin

Splendours of Qur'ān Calligraphy and Illumination. Vaduz, Liechtenstein: Thesaurus Islamicus Foundation, 2005.

    Striking color reproductions. A treasure-house of Koranic calligraphy.

Michon, Jean-Louis

Introduction to Traditional Islam: Foundations, Art, and Spirituality. Bloomington, IN: World Wisdom, 2008.

Fitzgerald, Michael and Judith

The Universal Spirit of Islam: From the Koran and Hadith. Bloomington, IN: World Wisdom, 2006.

    A rich and enlightening text accompanied by superb illustrations.

Grube, Ernst

The World of Islam. London: Paul Hamlyn, 1966.

Barrucand, Marianne and Bednorz, Achim

Moorish Architecture in Andalusia. Cologne: Taschen, 2002.

    Embellished with splendid photographs.

BIOGRAPHICAL NOTES

WILLIAM STODDART was born in Carstairs, Scotland, lived most of his life in London, England, and now lives in Windsor, Ontario. He studied modern languages, and later medicine, at the universities of Glasgow, Edinburgh, and Dublin. He was a close associate of both Frithjof Schuon and Titus Burckhardt during the lives of these leading perennialists and translated several of their works into English. For many years Stoddart was assistant editor of the British journal *Studies in Comparative Religion*. Pursuing his interests in comparative religion, he has traveled widely in Europe, North Africa, India, Sri Lanka, and Japan. Stoddart's works include *Outline of Hinduism* (1993; 2007 edition titled *Hinduism and Its Spiritual Masters*), *Outline of Buddhism* (1998), *Invincible Wisdom: Quotations from the Scriptures, Saints, and Sages of All Times and Places* (2008), *What Do the Religions Say About Each Other? Christian Attitudes towards Islam, Islamic Attitudes towards Christianity* (2008), and *What Does Islam Mean in Today's World?* (2012). His essential writings were published by World Wisdom as *Remembering in a World of Forgetting: Thoughts on Tradition and Postmodernism* (2008).

R.W.J. AUSTIN was born in 1938 in Willerby, Humberside, England. He received an Honors degree in Classical Arabic and a Ph.D. in Islamic Mysticism, both from the University of London. From 1963-1988 he taught Arabic and Islamic Studies in the School of Oriental Studies at the University of Durham. During this period he conducted research in Islamic mysticism in general and in the work of the renowned Sufi Muhyi 'd-Dīn Ibn 'Arabī (1165-1240) in particular. His works include a translation of Ibn Arabī's *Rūh al-Quds* ("The Spirit of Holiness") and extracts from *Ad-Durrat al-Fākhira* ("The Precious Jewel") under the title of *Sufis of Andalusia,* two treatises in which Ibn 'Arabī describes his meetings with the numerous Sufi masters whom he knew in his youth. Austin also translated important extracts from Ibn 'Arabī's *Fusūs al-Hikam* ("The Bezels of Wisdom") for the Classics of Western Spirituality series.

INDEX

Index

Pickthall, Marmaduke, 21
pilgrimage, 16, 17, 50, 51, 84.
    See also *hajj*
pork, 17
Potency, 5, 59, 62
Potentia, 60
poverty, 48, 56. See also *faqr*
prakriti, 59-60
prayer, 16, 20, 24, 27, 29, 41,
    45, 50-51, 53, 55-56, 75,
    82-83, 86
Prophet. *See* Mohammed, the
    Prophet
Prophetic Norm, 26, 74. See
    also *Sunna*
Psalms, 55
purusha, 59-60

Qādirī *tarīqa*, 45
qalb, 51
Quraish, 11

Rabb (Lord), 51
Rābi'a al-'Adawīya, 87
Rahma, 63
Ramadan, 17, 50
Rāmakrishna, 55
recitation, 11-12, 51
remembrance of God, 51,
    53, 74, 75, 82, 85. See also
    dhikr, invocation
revelation(s), 11, 13-14, 16,
    23, 26, 33, 34, 56, 67, 69
rosary, 51, 54, 75. See also
    wird
Rūh, 29, 30, 51
Rūmī, Jalāl ad-Dīn, 19, 45, 96

salām (peace), 51-52
salāt (ritual prayer), 16, 41,
    51-53

salvation, 1, 37, 41, 42, 65,
    67-68, 70
samsāra, 59
sanctity, 42, 44
sannyāsin (renunciate), 8
Sanskrit, 5, 11, 76
Sarah, 13
saum, 16, 51. *See also* fasting
Schimmel, Annemarie, 95
Schuon, Frithjof, xv, 13, 19,
    26, 34, 38, 44, 56, 73, 78,
    93
Seal of Prophecy, 18, 58
Seal of Sanctity, 18, 58
secularism, 15, 20
Semitic monotheisms, 7, 11,
    13
Shādhilī, Abū 'l-Hasan ash-,
    45, 48, 88
shahāda (witness), 16, 25-28,
    35, 49, 52, 53
Shah Jahan, Emperor, 37
Shakti, 59
Shankara, 71
sharī'a, 4-6, 16, 23, 33, 43,
    87. *See also* exoterism
Shī'a, 19, 93
Shī'is, Shī'ism, 19
Shinto, 7
Shiva, 59
shūdras, 8
Sikhism, 37
silk, 17
silsila (initiatic chain), 42,
    44, 47
soul, 29-32, 51, 55, 64, 69,
    89. See also *nafs*
Spain, Moorish, 94
spirituality, xiv, 1-3, 6, 31,
    34, 42, 49, 52, 67, 69,
    76-77

For a glossary of all key foreign words used in books published by World
Wisdom, including metaphysical terms in English, consult:
www.DictionaryofSpiritualTerms.org.
This on-line Dictionary of Spiritual Terms provides extensive definitions,
examples, and related terms in other languages.

Other Titles on Islam by World Wisdom

Art of Islam, Language and Meaning: Commemorative Edition,
by Titus Burckhardt, 2009

Christianity/Islam: Perspectives on Esoteric Ecumenism,
by Frithjof Schuon, 2008

Introduction to Sufi Doctrine,
by Titus Burckhardt, 2008

Introduction to Sufism: The Inner Path of Islam,
by Éric Geoffroy, 2010

Introduction to Traditional Islam, Illustrated:
Foundations, Art, and Spirituality,
by Jean-Louis Michon, 2008

Islam, Fundamentalism, and the Betrayal of Tradition:
Essays by Western Muslim Scholars,
edited by Joseph E.B. Lumbard, 2004, 2009

Maintaining the Sacred Center: The Bosnian City of Stolac,
by Rusmir Mahmutćehajić, 2011

Men of a Single Book:
Fundamentalism in Islam, Christianity, and Modern Thought,
by Mateus Soares de Azevedo, 2010

The Mystics of Islam,
by Reynold A. Nicholson, 2002

The Path of Muhammad: A Book on Islamic Morals
and Ethics by Imam Birgivi,
interpreted by Shaykh Tosun Bayrak, 2005

Paths to the Heart: Sufism and the Christian East,
edited by James S. Cutsinger, 2003